THE NEW YORKERS

THE
NEW YORKERS

A Profile of an American Metropolis

ANDREW HACKER

MASON / CHARTER

NEW YORK 1975

Library of Congress Cataloging in Publication Data

```
Hacker, Andrew.
   The New Yorkers.

   Includes bibliographical references.
   1.  New York (City)--Social conditions.  2.  Social
classes--New York (City)  I.  Title.
HN80.N5H16        309.1'747'1              75-4669
ISBN 0-88405-100-5
```

For Ann

Contents

1

Introducing Eight Million People

No single medium can convey New York. Reginald Marsh and Raphael Soyer, Leonard Bernstein and George M. Cohan— each has captured the city's cadence in a different way. A thousand movies and as many novels have shown how the rhythms of its streets shape the personality of its people. No one book can provide a full portrait. For this reason the current volume has a somewhat modest intention. It will seek to examine some of the qualities and characteristics of the 3,091,020 women, 2,569,023 men, and 2,234,819 children who, at the most recent count, live in New York City.

Accordingly there are certain subjects that will remain unexplored. For example, the organization of government and the city's economy will be alluded to but only as they affect the attitudes of individuals. Nor will the traditional topics, health, housing, and transportation, be analyzed. Matters such as these may safely be left to others. Books on the state of our cities will remain a publishing staple for some time to come. People are the focus of these pages, not programs or policies.

PROBLEMS IN PERSPECTIVE

Of course New York has problems. By virtually every accepted measure, it is deteriorating. Most of these signs reflect the changing character of the population: new people with a new

1

spirit of self-importance. At the same time, what happens in New York results from events elsewhere. The growth of suburbs, a changing technology, upheavals abroad—all affect the texture of the city. Yet if New York has become an unpalatable place for some people, for others it is a center of excitement and innovation they have purposely chosen. The task is not to draw up a balance sheet but to show how individuals differ in their conception of a city. Commonly cited statistics are susceptible to several interpretations.

Since 1950 New York has, for all intents and purposes, lost 2 million people. While its population remained constant (moving from 7,891,957 to 7,894,862 between 1950 and 1970), the nation as a whole grew by more than a third (going from 151,325,798 to 203,211,926). Had New York kept pace with the national growth rate it would have reached the 10 million mark by 1970. Quite obviously the city has lost much of its magnetism, which is bad for pride. People who once made New York their goal now go elsewhere. Families who prefer the suburbs now live there rather than settle for their second choice. Those who want sun and space move to Dallas and Phoenix and San Diego instead of grumbling about the cold and the crowding. Nevertheless, persons of all races and classes continue to move to New York. On the whole they come voluntarily: the city is what they want. In some cases it is their only alternative, but in more than a few instances they have several options but still choose New York. Better a smaller city but one with more people who live there because it offers a life they like.

In 1950 the police received reports of 2,350 robberies throughout the entire year. By 1973 the figure had climbed to 72,750, a thirtyfold increase even omitting unreported incidents. Compared with the past, New York is obviously far less safe, and no one will claim that more muggings make a better city. At the same time the upsurge in crime expresses a new sense of freedom on the part of classes which were once kept sternly in their place. Earlier generations maintained tight control over large segments of the population, particularly the poor. One consequence of relaxing these controls is an increase in crime.

In 1950 the fire department received 17,651 false alarms, of which 6,887 may have been honest mistakes. By 1974 they were running at an annual rate of 159,988, and the department had given up estimating how many were honest errors. False alarms are a form of vandalism, yet another symptom of a capriciousness pervading the city. Most are turned in by young people who feel entitled to outlets they see as expressing their individuality. Over the past decade New York has become a more youthful city and is probably the better for it. People into even their forties show much less of the stuffiness other periods praised as maturity. More New Yorkers enjoy themselves and with less embarrassment. Without realizing it they take many of their cues from the kids who turn in fire alarms.

As 1950 started, the welfare department had 264,750 people in its two largest programs—home relief and aid to families with dependent children—or one New Yorker in every 30. By 1974 the number of individuals on those rolls had risen to 970,000, or one out of eight city residents. That total included 640,000 children; 200,000 parents, mostly mothers; and about 100,000 mental patients, recently released prisoners, and individuals in addiction programs. The major reason for the almost fourfold increase in the welfare population is that fathers have fewer compunctions about walking out on their families and fewer people feel obliged to care for their bothersome relatives. Until the present generation, New Yorkers were more apt to endure loveless marriages, have grandma in the house, and put up with the arrival of unplanned children. People now think more of themselves and disown duties they once accepted. Yet the city gains as a creative center as citizens cut loose from burdens that dissipate their energies. Divorces, desertions, and other disclaimers of responsibility are hardly causes for congratulation, yet they mean that more people are thinking through how to put the most into their lives. Most heartening, perhaps, many now show signs of doing so before they become encumbered with obligations not easily abandoned later on.

In 1952 Lever Brothers dedicated its Park Avenue offices, establishing mid-Manhattan as a corporate capital. By 1955, according to the first *Fortune* listing, 39 of the largest 100 companies had New York headquarters. By 1973 only 27 of that group remained in the city. American Can had left for Greenwich, IBM went to Armonk, and Allied Chemical and American Cyanamid moved over to New Jersey. In a way, these shifts make sense. Corporations are essentially mid-American institutions; in large measure their success depends on keeping in touch with events far removed from Manhattan. A company might be better head-quartered in Pittsburgh or Akron or Wilmington, and many seem to prefer it that way. (Few executives who are assigned to New York offices choose to live in the city itself.) New York was never really meant to be a corporate town. Its strength lies in finance, communications, and the arts. A city cannot attain prominence in every area. Union Carbide and United States Steel are certainly welcome to stay, but, all things considered, their presence adds little to the city's character.

Within a four-year period, from 1969 to 1973, the city lost more than 250,000 jobs, of which almost 170,000 were in manufacturing. In 1950 New York accounted for almost 7 percent of the nation's industrial employment, with over half its population working at blue-collar jobs ranging from printing and apparel to baking and beer. By 1974 the city's share of factory employment had declined to half the 1950 figure. Any drop in employment is hardly an encouraging omen. The city still has people who need work. However, huge manufacturing plants now require land areas of the kind found only in a Lordstown, Ohio. New York cannot hope to be a factory city, given current industrial standards. At the same time, the work force has altered in another, less commented on, respect. In 1950 the employed population consisted of 2,202,713 men and 1,073,911 women, with the latter representing 38 percent of all women between 18 and 65. By 1970 the labor force contained 1,898,555 men and 1,292,815 women, meaning that more than half the city's women were employed. In the course of two decades more than 300,000 men disappeared from the work force, while the women's contingent increased by over 200,000. This interchange has contributed, perhaps more than any other single factor, to new attitudes and aspirations on the part of a gender which only a generation ago consisted mainly of housewives. In Manhattan, the center of this consciousness, 60 percent of the women residents have fulltime employment. (Subtracting black and Puerto Rican women, who are more apt to have young children, puts the proportion over 66 percent.) In addition, the fact that the majority are now at work influences the thinking of those still at home. Women now count for more in New York, and their presence is more strongly felt than in cities with expanding economies. Liberation is a post-industrial phenomenon.

By the indices most usually cited, New York is in a bad way. More of its citizens display selfish and destructive behavior, inflicting injuries on both themselves and one another. There was a time when every American community contained people who wanted to get to New York. The city now sends more persons down to South Carolina every year than it receives from that state. Even so, the statistics provide a one-dimensional picture. Despite the crime, vandalism, and its contracting economy, New York contains a more interesting collection of people than at any time in its history. There is more going on in terms of variety and self-enjoyment than in any urban center on this continent or most others. It is an adventuresome place to live for those who want that kind of life. And enough apparently do.

A CREATURE OF HISTORY

Everyone, regardless of ideology, agrees that the city has problems. Too many people lead half lives with little serious hope of relief. There was a time when observers persuaded themselves that all this could be changed. In universities, foundations, and research centers scholars had become convinced that their knowledge was reaching new peaks of understanding. More citizens had liberal arts educations, an experience tending to sympathy for theorizing. A city came to be seen as an "urban system." Its pavements would serve as proving grounds for a half-dozen disciplines to test their models. Computers, simulations, and the higher mathematics would all play a role. These, at least, were the assumptions of the experts of the 1960s:

New York offers a rich laboratory for fundamental urban research and a ripe, receptive, and supremely realistic stage for the application of operations research and computer-based methodology to urban problems.[1]

If we talk about the urban system rather than the urban scene, it is because we recognize that the city is a dynamic phenomenon, with many components interrelated with each other in very complex ways. We are interested in the city as a total system and believe we have the experience and potential capability to contribute towards an understanding of the urban system as a whole.[2]

As more subsystems are reliably treated in mathematical terms, it should be possible in time to combine several of them into an encompassing mathematical statement which retains descriptive and predictive validity. It may be possible eventually to arrive at an overall mathematical simulation which can be employed directly for comprehensive city planning.[3]

Automatic data processing allows us to deal analytically with realistic problems rather than oversimplified approximations. In this matter we will be able to develop a more thorough comprehension of the patterns and cycles of activity in the cities.[4]

Systems analysis is "what's happening" on the urban scene. Engineers are migrating from the space frontier to the urban frontier, and a new breed of socio-physical scientist has been born.[5]

Given this heralding, the scientific method could not confine itself simply to locating firehouses or routing garbage trucks. For a generation reared on sociology and conversant with psychoanalysis, old-line administration was not enough. Piers and playgrounds were all well and good, but the real problems rose from traits and tendencies within people themselves. Such citizens had to be reached and remotivated by bold programs which would change attitudes and open up opportunities.

The creation of new agencies and the renaming of old ones may signify very little. Even so, the way people describe their assignments can give a clue to their mental processes. The shift from "relief" to "welfare" to "social services" is a revealing one. It implies a change from simply keeping people alive, to aid in arranging their environment. Yet to go further—as has happened —and call the enterprise the administration of "human resources" suggests that people may be manipulable components in a system. Hence came programs whose very phrasing held hope for sweeping transformations: community enrichment, career development, model cities, environmental protection, family planning, addiction services, human rights, neighborhood youth corps, and, of course, community action. Many had federal funding. None existed 10 years earlier.

Later we will assess the impact of these and other programs, but at this point it will suffice to say that those who only a few years ago were proclaiming a new urban science now avow their disillusion. Few propose programs or, at least, with their oldtime abandon. Even fewer care to argue that computers or mathematical models can show us how to teach teenagers to read or reduce crime in the streets. The very people who said they could help the city with systems analysis are now attacking strip-mining or saving the caribou.

This is probably just as well. Cities are creatures of history. Governments cannot impose prosperity on a region. Events have a momentum of their own. The power to plan, let alone encourage, is small when set against unforeseen circumstances which move people and shape societies. Every age sees attempts to breathe new life into declining capitals. Yet even autocratic regimes find they cannot consign citizens to places they find uncongenial, and American governments have never sought such powers.

In 1840, New Orleans and Baltimore tied for the title of America's second city. Albany, Cincinnati, and Louisville numbered in the top dozen. In 1900 Scranton, St. Joseph, and Fall River had claims to metropolitan stature. Now the cities with a future are San Diego, Phoenix, and San Jose, with tracts of territory so vast as to be chiefly suburban in character. The fate of a city is tied to countless decisions that are difficult to detect and impossible to control. Landlords and legislators, engineers and investors, operate occasionally in concert, often at cross-purposes, with the best laid of plans altered by events across an ocean or on another continent.

We cannot know what will happen to New York over the coming decades. The generation now being reared in the suburbs may decide that they have had enough of lawns and station wagons to last their lifetime. But this need not mean they will head for New York. A yet undiscovered Aspen or Taos may be more to their liking. On the other hand, the city could undergo a commercial renaissance. For it is attracting large numbers of newcomers with a taste for entrepreneurship. Cubans and Haitians, Thais and Puerto Ricans, Japanese and Dominicans, have business talents unlike any the city has seen in years. (It should be remembered that for almost half a century, from 1913 to 1960 or so, New York received hardly any immigrants from abroad.) Their presence could make the city into a center of shops and services for an expanding series of clienteles. One change seems more than a passing fashion, however; put very simply, New Yorkers of all descriptions want fewer children. Many want none at all, and most have no pressing desire to become parents. Recent figures tell this story.

In 1951, 162,755 babies were delivered in the city, or 20 per thousand people in the population. In 1973, New Yorkers produced 111,410 infants, down to 14 per thousand, a birthrate decline of 30 percent. Other statistics are no less striking. Within only a two-year period, 1971 to 1973, the number of babies born to mothers on welfare dropped from 23,643 to 17,704. This decline of 25 percent was steeper than that registered by the city as a whole. And in the single year 1973, 172,985 abortions were performed in New York. Some involved out-of-town visitors, but not nearly so many as in the past, given the increasing availability of abortions throughout the country. Even if only 60 percent of the women were resident New Yorkers, this would mean that there were more abortions than live births in the city.

There are a variety of reasons why people do not want children or postpone having them or limit their number. In the past the issue tended to come down to having enough food on the table for an expanding brood. Now, in an age of more sophisticated tastes, the question turns on college fees, summer camps, and other investments in personal development. With children so heavily capitalized, even well-heeled couples will stop at two.

Yet there is another, less mentioned, reason which has particular relevance to New York. Not so long ago childless couples were often called "selfish." In a way, this accusation was accurate, for most parents realize that the joys of having children seldom equal the costs. Parenthood imposes limits on a person's life for at least a 20-year period. Having children prevents a couple from doing countless things they might otherwise enjoy. (A 1973 survey updating Kinsey showed that even couples in their late twenties and early thirties have sex less than three times a week; the presence of children is the chief reason for the limited ration.[6]) New York now has more young people who wish to prolong the pleasures they now know. Perhaps this is a sign of selfishness; on the other hand, no one proposes today that people have a duty to reproduce. One might argue that hedonism weakens the spirit, whereas sacrifice strengthens character. Still, there must be more rational avenues for self-denial than adding more offspring to an overcrowded world.

At all events, the city appears likely to have fewer children. One result may be a reduction of those exuberances usually associated with youth. Crime rates, vandalism, even false alarms, will decrease simply by attrition. The 168,383 children who were born in 1961 make up a pool which by 1978 will contribute a disquieting number of delinquents. However, as the city had only 111,140 births in 1973, citizens who stick it out until 1990 may look forward to substantially fewer depredations.

The real point is that New York will be composed increasingly of people intent on enjoying themselves. Some will be younger individuals who settle for quite modest incomes due to simpler diversions. Many college graduates will continue with conventional professions. Others will be content to drive a taxicab from time to time or wait on tables. The city will also have an older generation of single people, some between marriages and others done with such arrangements. It will show greater variety in its sexual expression. As New York becomes a more homosexual city—more of a woman's city, a more adulterous city—not just tolerance but an enhanced understanding will emerge.

These developments have contributed to the prominence of what will be called in this book the "cosmopolitan" class of New Yorkers. Before proceeding, it would be well to direct a few words to the question of classes in New York, particularly in light of the emphasis on ethnicity that pervades nearly all discussions of the city.

CLASSES AND CHARACTER

Race, religion, and national origin are facts of urban life. One obviously cannot describe a city without alluding to color or other ethnic strains. So let us grant the "importance" of such factors at the outset. A person's origins involve much of his identity, partly because he so sees himself, partly because others so see him. All of us use such shorthand, if only to save time. To say that the psychiatrist was Jewish, the mugger was black, or the construction worker was Italian sums up our message. (Had the mugger been Jewish, the psychiatrist Italian, or the construction worker black, we would need additional paragraphs to elucidate the story.) What follows in this book will allude to ethnicity wherever that factor seems relevant, but it will not be over-stressed.

New York has more than its share of spokesmen ready to expound on the black experience, the Puerto Rican heritage, the Mediterranean tradition, more than enough observers to worry aloud about Chinese youth gangs, Jewish poverty, and elderly Anglo-Saxons. The fact that the city has citizens of Haitian or Hungarian or Hellenic ancestry seems sufficient to set in motion yet one more program for celebrating another round of neglected contributions. Ethnicity has become one of New York's major industries, not least because it plays on guilt feelings of the assimilated and a politics pledged to keeping everyone happy.

All this obviously deflects attention from other kinds of clusterings which may, if examined, provide a more profound understanding of the city. In particular, New York can be seen as an arrangement of classes which cut across variations of hue and heritage. Americans have always been reluctant to see their society as having such a structure. *Classes* suggest conflict, hier-archy, and barriers that can be overcome only by unusual effort. Other nations may have such a system, but ours, we tell ourselves, is an open society, hence the ethnic euphemisms. Instead of pondering those traits that make the middle-class averse to com-mingling with the poor, we draw maps and mentalities in terms of colors, a substitution as unfair as it is misleading. The problems we call racial discrimination, school integration, and neighbor-hood deterioration can all be analyzed as mutations of class differ-ences.

A city of classes. . . . The Marxian demarcations won't do, or at least not in the current era. Any attempt to separate the population into a bourgeoisie and a proletariat, into propertied and propertyless, into exploiters and exploited, runs into endless difficulties. Of course the city has workers, many of whom willingly acknowledge membership in a working class. Yet even with unions, strikes, and antipathy for their employers, New Yorkers show few symptoms of a proletarian consciousness. If asked to identify the chief adversaries in their lives, most will point either to politicians or to fellow citizens of another color. A contorted perception of reality, perhaps, but it is their mentality and is expressive of our time.

New York has property-owners. They range from retired couples who own a tenement or two to proprietors of grocery stores and garment lofts and on to families of inherited wealth and accumulated fortunes. But most New Yorkers work for corporate organizations, whether business or governmental, and most bosses are salaried executives who have no ownership interest of consequence. (The closest approximation to the classical bourgeoisie are the city's real estate barons. But even they, with David Rockefeller added, do not comprise a class.) America still has a capitalist economy, and property still plays a crucial role in the city, but the people in presiding positions are agents of an impersonal system. Were a hundred board chairmen to be expropriated tomorrow, the edifice would continue running much as it always has. The classes of the city are not to be found in its property arrangements.

Another, more recent, approach also deserves some attention. Edward Banfield, probably the most straightforward student of American cities, defines classes in terms of attitudes they hold toward the future. The higher one's class, the more he is apt to eschew ephemeral pleasures, to think of the years ahead and assume that adherence to social rules will bring due rewards. These classes still accept large parts of the puritan ethic or its earlier version, the grasshopper and the ant. The lower one descends in the class system, the more he lives from moment to moment. Here Banfield has ruffled a lot of liberal feathers. "Impulse governs his behavior," he says of the lower-class citizen, "either because he cannot discipline himself . . . or because he has no sense of the future."[7]

Many people who are born poor continue to strive anyway, even in deadend jobs paying marginal wages. According to Banfield such persons should not be considered lower class. By the same token he withholds the upper class designation from play-boys who run through their trust funds. What this means, then, is that the analysis turns on *character* rather than *class*. Every society contains some who display strength of character and others who are weak of will. On the whole we know little about the formation of human fiber. (Of course every educationist and psychoanalyst has a theory—their professions expect it of them.) Birth and upbringing give some citizens a social shielding that ensures survival without undue hardship or testing. Privilege always protects the well-born weak. In the final analysis most of us are probably closer to the grasshopper end of the spectrum. When poor people succumb to impulse, they suffer heavy penalties. For the middle class, momentary indulgence may compromise a marriage or make it necessary to renew a bank loan, but it seldom jeopardizes one's entire life.

Banfield's writings warrant serious reflection because he touches on topics too often left unconsidered. Just as commentators tend to avoid questions of class, so they also prefer to circumvent the issue of character. Even granting social conditioning and parental influences, behavior still reflects basic traits of unclear origins. Most people are not particularly strong or persevering or impervious to temptations. Indeed, New York may be understood as a city geared to consumption rather than production, to enjoying immediate experiences rather than pondering its long-term future.

Sociologists have several indexes for categorizing people, the best known focusing on income, education, and occupation. Attainments in these areas tend to run along parallel paths. A high school diploma, for example, usually leads to certain kinds of jobs having a certain income range. Nevertheless, there are enough exceptions—from self-made executives to well-educated bartenders—to upset any simple scheme. Even if we could assign everyone to a tier, it could still omit attributes which contribute most to individuals' identities. Placing a person in the "lower middle class" often implies that he has distinctive tastes or attitudes. At the time of the 1970 Census, Brooklyn had 81,014 families with incomes between $10,000 and $12,000 a year. Is anyone willing to generalize about the values held by people in that stratum? Queens contains 52,225 women who attended, but never completed, college; no creditable scholar would try to capsulize their outlooks on the strength of that datum. Adding other variables obviously helps. Home ownership, the school one's children attend, whether relatives live nearby, may help round out a picture. Yet even after recording these and other factors we may discover that one person spends most of his time drinking beer with the boys while his neighbor sets out for Avery Fisher Hall at every opportunity.

As a concept, class is a cross between a nettle and a mulberry bush. We keep circling round and round yet can never grasp it with confidence. Our intuitions may tell us that New York does in fact have classes, yet the information we have at hand—indeed, our very powers of perception—seem inadequate for delineating them. Hence the recourse to ethnic designations, on the assumption that these, in themselves, tell a story. Perhaps they do, but we should be able to do better. At least, an attempt is in order.

Chapter 2 will cover the conventional categories, to determine how the city divides along economic, occupational, and educational lines. (It will also chart changes over a 20-year period, to give some perspective to current distributions.) This information cannot, in itself, create classes, but it can help establish the context out of which that understanding may come. For example, it is relevant to know that (again in 1970) New York had 139,775 households with incomes over $25,000. This does not mean that everyone in that bracket had *upper middle class* interests of a specifiable sort, but it does silhouette the pool of people from whom certain affinities may be expected.

In another chapter we will explore political behavior in recent years. The ways citizens cast their ballots often tells us something about how they perceive both themselves and their city. Preferences for particular candidates do not, in themselves, reflect social classes. Nevertheless, electoral outlooks can express sentiments running a good deal deeper than who should sit in City Hall. How people vote has some parallels with their social standing. Again, there are too many cases in which someone with all the expected attributes ends up on the unexpected side.

The remaining chapters rely less on traditional data, for, in largest measure, class is a matter of values. There are various ways to live in a city like New York. Some people have few options, or circumstances deprive them of choices. The alcoholic whose existence turns on the next pint bottle. Addicts and ex-addicts, perpetually in and out of programs, who cannot hold a job for two weeks running. Old women slumped in doorways, their worldly goods in shopping bags. Or those prepared to prey on others for small change or more ambitious takings. All are New Yorkers and all see their city in a certain way. One question is whether the harsh economics and the continual insecurity of poverty prevent a person from taking an expansive view of his surroundings. Can a mother trying to support three children on a welfare check know a life in New York that is in any way distinctive from the one she would find in Toledo? To most in the lower depths, one city may be indistinguishable from another. Still, one hears of teenagers and grandmothers with hardly more than two tokens in their pockets who have come to know the entire length of the city. They roam beyond their immediate neighborhoods, finding a variety of diversions: watching an ocean liner dock, listening to opera in the park, bicycling across two boroughs to an unexplored beach. The poor do have problems, not the least of which is that so many of them never get to know their city.

But the divide of most moment involves classes of at least moderate means. At issue here are divergent conceptions of how best to spend one's days, of the most salutary setting for the good life. A distinction can be drawn between *neighborhood* and *cosmopolitan* New Yorkers. Moreover, these groups will be seen as classes whose membership cuts across considerations of race and income. Some neighborhood people have tastes that take them to rarefied parts of the city. A cosmopolitan citizen may direct much of his energies to activities close to home. Perhaps the demarcation has mainly to do with whether what you want most from life can be found only in a world capital or whether you could, in fact, see yourself living contentedly in any one of a hundred suburbs or cities. It has already been suggested that at least some historical forces will benefit the cosmopolitan conception, particularly the increased tendency to postpone parenthood. Also, neighborhood New Yorkers find their desire for safe and well-tended territory threatened by families whose advent brings peeling paint and overflowing garbage cans. Millions of neighborhood people have already left the city, especially as nearby schools enroll pupils with delinquent or disruptive tendencies. On the other hand, the cosmpolitan class has been augmented with the arrival of people who choose New York because its very vibrancy expresses part of their personality.

Classes come in conflict. The tensions need not be explicitly Marxian, but they can still involve a struggle for dominance. At least one recent election seemed to array neighborhood against cosmopolitan New Yorkers over which values the city should emphasize. That contest revolved around a figure who symbolized some of the basic rifts in the city; indeed, his presence affected citizens of every description.

NEW YORKERS AND THE LINDSAY ERA

The greater part of this book will concentrate on John Lindsay's two terms as New York City's 103rd mayor. However, the successes and failures of that tenure must receive their reckoning elsewhere. The chief concern of these pages will be less the magistrate in City Hall than the people who made up his constituency. The years 1965 through 1973 will be remembered as John Lindsay's era. How citizens reacted to that interlude throws light on a changing city.

John Lindsay set his imprint on New York as firmly as had Fiorello LaGuardia a generation earlier. One should not hold one man responsible for all that happened during his period in office. It would be too easy to suggest that Lindsay urged individuals to go on welfare, as it would be to imply that he encouraged others to choose crime as an avocation. Citizens like to blame elected officials for every woe of the social order. Even where developments cannot be attributed to those in office—graffiti, pornography, snowfalls—they are still expected to produce swift and sweeping remedies. Official action can, of course, make an impact. Changes in transit fares, a redeployment of police personnel, or revisions of the building code inevitably have an effect, but less than people would like to think.

So far as New York was concerned, changes during Lindsay's years in office stemmed less from his magistracy than from the uncoordinated activities of eight million people as they led their everyday lives. The era's history was made by a South Bronx father when he walked out on his wife and children, by a Brooklyn businessman who moved his plant to New Jersey, by a Queens couple's decision to postpone becoming parents so they could stay in the city a little longer.

Lindsay's first term began just as the 1960s passed their midpoint, a decade that opened with John Kennedy's promise of a New Frontier. This was the period when civil rights turned into black power; when Columbia University exploded, but Harlem did not. It was when Bloomingdale's and *New York* magazine became established institutions, while Brooklyn Heights showed how imagination could bring new life to an old area. These years saw people of all ages and classes affirming opinions and identities: women, homosexuals, and spouses of both sexes sought a freedom once known only by a favored few. Thirty thousand residents of the Bronx made a commitment to New York by buying apartments in Co-op City, a sign of affluence as well as an earnest of allegiance. Salaries and stock prices rose to new heights during Lindsay's tenure, expanding expectations just as a grimmer inflation and downturn would arrive later. These years belonged to the Mets, Rangers, and Knicks, to *Village Voice* and Channel 13. Even the upsurge of crime expressed new ideas about probity and property, just as drugs challenged conventional boundaries of experience. In short, whole segments of the population reexamined both their status in the city and their aspirations as individuals.

John Lindsay's presence in Gracie Mansion awakened the consciousness of people who might otherwise have stayed with the mood and mentality of earlier eras. During this eight-year period whole classes of individuals became more assertive than they had ever been in the past. On the whole New Yorkers were relatively undemanding as citizens before 1965. They may have displayed a defensiveness in their personalities; living in so compacted a setting evokes this. Yet until the Lindsay years they tended to ask little of their government, just as they settled for modest vistas in their private lives.

These revised self-estimates were not confined to New York, but the tenor of its life underwent more penetrating changes than

took place in other cities. John Lindsay contributed to this difference. Urban administrations elsewhere tended to maintain low
profiles, preferring to rely on established agencies and work
through traditional coalitions. In New York from 1965 to 1973
countless citizens apparently believed that the time was ripe to
vent grievances and assert ambitions. Lindsay's own outlook
seemed to indicate that life could and would become better,
fuller, more satisfying and exciting. While those promises were
seldom explicit ("Fun City"?), his very person carried that message. Moreover, New Yorkers were ready for John Lindsay. Sentiments he would arouse already lay near the surface. The demography of the city was beginning to fashion the contours of a new
civic personality.

Eight million people, then, form the subject of these pages:
its heroes and heroines, villains and victims. If the chapters that
follow show a population divided into camps and classes, they also
point to traits possessed by the entire citizen body. Despite variations in incomes and origins, plus an increasingly polarized politics, New Yorkers of all classes and colors share several underlying
outlooks. Compared either with their predecessors in the past or
citizens elsewhere on this globe, the people of New York have a
more orotund conception of their worth than any population in
history.

These presumptions make New York a far livelier place than
Chicago or Los Angeles or any comparable center. New Yorkers
show a fondness for their own opinions, a penchant for public
pronouncements, an adeptness in the obstructive arts. John Lindsay's own approach to life helped to encourage these bruitings;
his office gave them a legitimacy normally denied by urban executives. During those eight years, eight million people came to feel
that they mattered.

Where did they come from? The next chapter will set the
stage by profiling the changes in New York's population over
recent decades. This is the first study of New York to use Census
materials in so wideranging a way. (None of the tables in the
chapter have appeared in official documents; in all cases their
preparation required special computations.) For the most part,
Chapter 2 uses 1950 and 1970 as decennial benchmarks. Figures
from the earlier census give a glimpse of a day when the city had

quite different characteristics. The eight years 1965–73 were too short a span for significant demographic change. What the Census can show, by charting a 20-year period, is how the population had developed by the midpoint of Lindsay's tenure.

2

A Portrait in Percentages

Even in a supposedly scientific age most of us remain somewhat skeptical about quantification. We worry lest flesh and blood be reduced to statistical skeletons or that researchers will focus on the parts of problems for which they have figures, to the neglect of more critical questions. Rigorous methodologies have a use in certain areas, but the important issues of our time depend on an intuitive understanding, on insights we cannot always explain to ourselves, let alone to others.

Even so, statistics have augmented our knowledge and in ways that are not entirely pedestrian. Numbers never tell the whole story, but if carefully chosen they can serve as compass points for an uncertain voyage. Moreover, columns of figures often reveal regularities—or even surprises—unnoticed by experienced observers. This chapter will portray New York City from the vantage point of the United States Census. Tabulations of this sort have several virtues. For one thing, the Census is about as comprehensive a survey as we are entitled to expect. For another, its reports are public property. Thus, while there will always be arguments over interpretation, the availability of the original data means that we can check one another's analyses for basic accuracy. (An analysis of Census accuracy and other questions concerning its use are contained in Appendix II.)

The mills at the Census grind slowly, mainly because they are so meticulous. New Yorkers handed in their forms in April 1970, yet even as 1973 came to an end not all the figures had been

19

published. The question is not whether statistics become out-dated (they obviously do) but whether recent changes have vitiated their usefulness. There seems some reason to believe that the first half of the 1970s was not as fast-paced a time for the city as earlier years. Migration into and out of New York has slowed down, birthrates have fallen off, and people apparently changed jobs less often. Due to a strident inflation, real income did not advance by any great bounds in the post-Census period. The distribution of earnings and wealth has probably remainly fairly constant. However, the family incomes reported by the Census need periodic upgrading to reflect new wage levels, even if purchasing power remains unchanged.

The principal method of this chapter is to compare the Census findings of 1970 with their counterpart figures from 1950. The earlier reports portray a New York of a different era. When people say that the city has changed, they as often as not contrast it with the place they knew a generation ago. The 1950 Census shows the city before the large migrations from the southern states and Caribbean countries and before the great outflow to the suburbs. Those two decades pretty much embrace the span we think of as the "postwar period." Data for the city will occasionally be contrasted with figures for suburbs or the country as a whole. If New York changed between 1950 and 1970 it would be well to compare this change with happenings elsewhere. Finally, materials from sources other than the Census will be used if they provide a useful supplement.

GENERATIONS

In one major respect New York has been a model city, having maintained a zero population growth through the last two Censuses. Between 1950 and 1970 the city's population rose from 7,891,957 to 7,895,563—an increase of only 3,606, or four one-hundredths of 1 percent. This stability makes New York exceptional when set against other urban centers. Among the 10 next largest cities in 1950, only semisuburban Los Angeles did not suffer a population decline during the succeeding decades. Boston, Cleveland, Detroit, and St. Louis, for example, all lost more than a fifth of their residents during the period. To be sure, New York was standing still while the country as a whole was growing. Had the city managed to keep pace with the national growth rate of 34 percent, it would have had a population of 10,619,347 by 1970. By the standards of urban America, New York's stability has been unusual. Most cities cannot attract enough new arrivals to replace their daily departures.

Among the 58 American cities with 1970 populations exceeding 250,000—which includes places like Akron and Jersey City—no fewer than 49 experienced relative or absolute declines during the preceding decade. Of these, 38 actually lost numbers and the other 11 fell behind the national growth rate. Even newer cities such as Denver, Seattle, Tulsa, and Tampa registered their 1970 populations in red ink. The nine successful cities all stretch along the country's sun belt from Miami to San Jose, with Houston, Dallas, El Paso, Phoenix, and San Diego dotting the corridor. These cities tend to have room for expansion and are as much suburban as urban in atmosphere. Houston sprawls over 434 square miles, an area equal to Westchester county. San Diego has more space than Boston, Philadelphia, and Detroit combined.

If New York's head count remained constant, its internal composition underwent significant changes. The 1970 Census found the city both younger and older than it had been in 1950. By 1970 New York contained more youngsters than at any time in its history. Compared with 1950, it had 322,174 additional children in its streets and schools. The birthrate has declined dramatically since the 1970 Census, so the current generation of youngsters may be the last of its size for some time to come. Even so, the 1970 count had 142 girls and boys between the ages of five and nine for every 100 adults aged 35 to 39. In other words, New York has an ample supply of children for the next few decades.

The city also gained 342,643 elderly citizens between 1950 and 1970. In 1950 one New Yorker in 13 was 65 or older; by 1970 one in eight was that age. Put another way, the number of old people rose by 57 percent between the two censuses. For the United States as a whole the aged part of the population increased at a greater rate than it did in New York. In fact, smaller

Table 2.1. Generations

	1950		1970	
Under 18	1,912,645	24%	2,234,819	28%
18 to 29	1,462,910	19	1,485,459	19
30 to 64	3,911,167	50	3,226,706	41
65 and over	605,235	7	947,878	12
	7,891,957	100%	7,894,862	100%

towns have more older people than do large cities. In upstate Middletown and Canajoharie the proportion of the population over 65 approaches one citizen in five. On the other hand, the 30-to-64 age bracket fell by 684,461 persons in New York during the 20 years. Interestingly, this decline embraced not only young parents with school-age children but also people in their fifties who became commuters or left the area altogether.

ETHNICITY

For most people the word *change* usually connotes color. Like all other cities, New York became more darkly complected. Between 1950 and 1970 the city's black population more than doubled, from 747,608 to 1,665,470, while a million whites left for the suburbs or more distant places. Even so, New York remains among the most Caucasian of American cities. Amid its companions in the 1950 top 10, only Los Angeles has fewer black residents relative to its population. Chicago, Cleveland, and Philadelphia all are more than 30 percent black. For Baltimore and Detroit the proportion exceeds 40 percent.

Classifications by skin color account for only part of the

Table 2.2. Ethnicity: Three Categories

	1950		1970	
White	7,116,441	90%	6,051,442	77%
Black	747,608	10	1,665,470	21
Other	27,908	—	177,906	2
	7,891,957	100%	7,894,818	100%

tan even though the borough lost population during that period.

The Census does not detail how many people each state sent to the city, but it does provide this information for the entire metropolitan area, and in that area the city accounts for 61 percent of the in-migrations. We have no way of knowing what proportion of those arriving from, say, Indiana, went to the city and how many journeyed directly to one of the suburbs. Nevertheless, the information has a story of its own that is worth recording.

The metropolitan area received 362,856 people between 1965 and 1970, whereas 888,316 of its residents left during that period, a ratio of 245 departures for every 100 persons entering the region. Upstate New York, plus contiguous Connecticut, Massachusetts, Pennsylvania, and New Jersey, contributed 162,861 people, or 45 percent of the in-migrants. The 11 southern states—North Carolina, Virginia, South Carolina, Texas, Georgia, Alabama, Louisiana, Tennessee, Mississippi, Arkansas, and Florida—sent only 79,667 people, which came to 22 percent of the intake. The remaining 34 states represented a wide scattering, ranging from 25,522 Californians who gave up their sun and sand for New York's soot and slush, to 930 from Nebraska and 107 from Wyoming (see Appendix I).

Emigration made for a more varied pattern. Upstate New York and the four contiguous states accounted for 436,473, or 49 percent of the departures. Florida by itself beckoned 124,020 people, or 14 percent of the total, while the other southern states got 85,968, or 10 percent, among them. California led the rest of the country, drawing 81,654 ex-New Yorkers. Nebraska attracted 1,338, and Wyoming got 364.

Even without counting Florida, the southern states drew more people from the New York area (85,968) than they sent in return (62,598). Only 1,654 came from Mississippi and a mere 593 from Arkansas. Among the other states, only Iowa managed to attract fewer New Yorkers (1,543) compared with the number it shipped out (1,672). The out-migrations to California and Florida make the most striking figures. Their total of 205,674 surpassed by almost 25,000 the entire outward surge to the Connecticut and New Jersey suburban fringe.

DOMESTIC ARRANGEMENTS

New York is less a family city than ever in the past. It contains fewer married couples, and more of its young adults live apart from their parents. In 1970 single people who occupied apartments of their own or shared them with roommates accounted for a third of the city's households. (In Manhattan they made up close to half.) While it is true that more of the city's families are now childless or have only one parent present, the growth of single-parent households should not be overstressed. Despite the recent focus on fatherless households, that condition is less novel than many commentators suggest and was already pronounced in 1950. At that time 19 percent of New York's families were headed by a single adult, not very different from the 21 percent in 1970. The increase in concern came more from a change in life-styles than the rise in numbers. In 1950 most of the women heading those households worked in ill-paid jobs, whereas in 1970 they were more likely to receive public stipends. In addition, the children of fatherless families caused less trouble in that generation and were generally less obtrusive even though their parents were gone all day.

Single individuals now play a much more prominent role in the city's demography. In 1950 sons and daughters tended to remain at home until they got married, due partly to the shortage of apartments but also because at that time young adults still saw themselves as members of the family. Between 1950 and 1970, New York's stock of homes and apartments rose by 20 percent, from 2,433,456 to 2,924,384 units, even though the population remained stable. Despite all the abandonments in Brownsville and the South Bronx, New Yorkers have more places to live and are less crowded in them. Since 1950 the average tenancy per

Table 2.5. Domestic Arrangements

	1950	1970	Change
Married couples living together	1,874,525	1,634,508	−13%
Families headed by a single adult	402,215	440,378	+10
Single persons living alone	735,285	986,566	+34
Widowed and divorced persons	638,636	771,670	+21

apartment has declined from 3.1 persons to 2.6 persons. The chief reason for this density decrease is the upsurge in one or two single individuals living alone or sharing an apartment. Indeed, well over half of the new units added to the city's housing supply were created for just such tenants.

Furthermore, New Yorkers pay about the same amount for their housing as they did a generation ago. In 1950 the median rental came to $43 per month, or 17 percent of the median household income of $3,073. In 1970 the median rental had risen to $109, which was still 17 percent of the $7,679 median income. Even with the relaxation of rent controls and the rise of luxury buildings, the cost of housing remained constant. Moreover, New York's rents are still modest compared with those of other cities. In Chicago the median stood at $121 in 1970, in Boston the figure was $126, and the average San Francisco renter paid $135. Even upstate residents in Syracuse and Rochester turned over more to their landlords than did their New York counterparts.

EDUCATION AND EMPLOYMENT

Census figures for education, employment, and income all show that by 1970 New York had become substantially a middle-class city. Twenty years earlier only a modest fraction of its residents had qualified for middle-class status, at least in terms of the characteristics usually used for that purpose. In 1950 only 12 percent of all New Yorkers aged 25 or over had attended college, while more than two-thirds had not even completed high school. By 1970 the number who had had at least some experience of college had reached 889,414, or almost 20 percent of the adult residents of the city. Moreover, this growth occurred despite the addition to the city's population of several hundred thousand persons from southern states and the Caribbean countries, settings not particularly noted for their encouragement of education.

Even so, New York's educational advances lagged behind those of the country as a whole. If the number of New Yorkers who completed college grew from 368,980 to 506,653, a rise of 57 percent, between 1950 and 1970, throughout the United

Table 2.6. Education[a]

	1950		1970	
Four or more years of college	368,980	7%	506,653	11%
One to three years of college	273,320	5	382,761	8
Four years of high school	1,083,465	21	1,350,764	28
Less than four years of high school	3,451,860	67	2,534,838	53
	5,177,625	100%	4,775,016	100%

[a]Persons aged 25 and older.

States the number of individuals finishing college increased by 83 percent. In 1950 New York held 7 percent of America's college graduates; by 1970 it accounted for a little more than 4 percent. Before the suburbs began expanding, New York and other large cities were the major middle-class centers of the nation. Now that class is much more dispersed. Thus, while the urban middle class is larger than at any time in its history, it tends to be ignored because of the focus on economic and educational advances in the suburbs.

The experience with employment has followed a parallel path. In 1950 a total of 3,276,624 New Yorkers held jobs. By 1970 the figure was 3,191,370, an absolute decline of 85,254. These figures and those which follow refer to employed residents of the city, regardless of where they happen to work; as it turns out, 95 percent of them work within the city itself. A total of 576,419 non-New Yorkers commuted to jobs in the city in 1970, but they are not under discussion here.

The fact that the city has fewer employment opportunities is well known. The number of available positions continues to decrease and will probably go on doing so for some years to come. The reason is that goods and services which used to be produced only or mostly in New York are now being produced in a multiplicity of places. Whereas once only New York had certain skills, other areas have developed equivalent talents.

But in another sense, there has been no employment decline at all. In 1950 the city had 5,254,960 residents of working age (18 to 65), and of these, 61 percent held jobs. In 1970 the working-age population had declined to 4,593,048, of which 68 percent were employed. By this measure more New Yorkers support themselves than did in the past. One reason for this advance lay in the new sexual ratio of the employment force. Between 1950 and 1970 the number of working women rose by 218,904 while men in the labor force declined by 304,158. By the latter year 4 in every 10 New York job-holders were women. Half of the city's women held jobs, and 42 percent of the mothers with children aged 6 through 17 were employed. This shift shows that the city created more of the kinds of jobs that are usually assigned to women, particularly in office work; it also means that New York has fewer women whose major occupation is being a housewife.

Another change has to do with job categories. During the two decades the city lost 333,471 blue-collar positions and gained 233,765 clerical jobs, reflecting familiar transitions in the economy. The loss of 20,457 sales workers can be explained by the shift to self-service and the tendency of more people holding such positions to commute from the suburbs. But more striking is the gain of 164,112 professional persons and the loss of no less than 129,203 individuals the Census classes as managers, administrators, or proprietors. The latter loss occurred despite the growth of administrative positions in public service and nonprofit organizations, even though small retail establishments seem as pervasive as in the past, with each one having its own proprietor. The significant development is that fewer New Yorkers work for businesses or think of themselves as businessmen. Even people who belong to commercial organizations are more apt to identify themselves as professionals. This is also true in public employment, where more of the newly created positions tend to be professional, as in health and education. In this sense New York

Table 2.7. Employment

	1950		1970	
Sales	253,305	8%	232,848	7%
Managers and proprietors	379,395	12	250,192	8
Professional and technical	338,060	10	502,172	16
Clerical	629,906	19	863,671	27
Nonwhite collar	1,675,958	51	1,342,487	42
	3,276,624	100%	3,191,370	100%

is less a business city, with fewer of its residents thinking in terms of balance sheets or profit and loss. Insofar as tastes, styles, and dispositions evoked by professional occupations differ from those desired in business jobs, the whole atmosphere of the city may reflect its changed employment panorama.

Another consequence of the growth in clerical and professional positions is that people travel farther to work. In 1960, 57 percent of Brooklyn's residents worked in their home borough; in 1970, only 49 percent did. The proportion of people both living and working on Staten Island declined from 56 percent to 47 percent during that decade. In the city as a whole the number of people traveling to jobs in a different borough rose by 384,097, or 22 percent. This change came mainly from the closing of factories in the outer boroughs and the expansion of Manhattan office jobs, which also explains the shifting sexual ratio in employment. Among the 153,486 New Yorkers who journeyed to jobs outside the city in 1970, most went to Nassau county (54,896), followed by New Jersey (42,426) and Westchester (30,513). In addition, 652 New Yorkers told the Census that they worked in California, and 146 listed Texas.

Finally, according to the 1970 census, the largest single number of people (1,390,517) took the subway to work. They were followed by those using cars (803,626), busses (461,271), feet (297,132), taxicabs (37,780), and railroads (30,847). A further group (27,851) listed "other," which presumably includes ferries, helicopters, and hansom carriages. An additional 57,146 New Yorkers worked at home.

INCOMES, EARNED AND UNEARNED

Discussion of income has a capacity for arousing controversy beyond any associated with education or occupations. People can be categorized according to their years of schooling or type of job fairly easily. Try, however, to reach agreement on the annual income a family must have to no longer be considered poor. Or try polling people on the dollar figures that set upper and lower limits to the "middle class." The problems are obvious and have been much discussed. Crane operators make more than college professors. Young people with low earnings may have more elevated tastes than their affluent elders. One family with a $100,000 income still seems middle class, while another appears rich. Yet for all these disagreements, the distribution of income remains an indispensable index for understanding a city. Wealth is still the major determinant of social class, even if other factors play significant roles. Money never tells the whole story, but it is the longest chapter.

The arrangement to be used here will divide New York's households into three economic groups. The decision to use three classes rather than four or five is entirely arbitrary, as are the dividing lines that separate the strata. These "classes" refer only to income. A Yale graduate earning $95 a week as a bookstore clerk goes into the lowest grouping; a headwaiter who clears $25,000 is included in the highest category.

Between 1950 and 1970 important changes occurred in the city's income structure. But before detailing those shifts, a few points must be clarified. Due to inflation over that two-decade period, the dollar's purchasing power depreciated by approximately 50 percent. Thus a household needed $15,000 in 1970 to buy goods and services that would have cost $10,000 20 years earlier. For this reason different figures delineate the respective classes for the two years. In addition, the Census calls every income unit a "household," which, in turn, refers either to a family or an "unrelated individual." A family consists of two or more relatives, which means that two sisters would qualify. In contrast, an unrelated individual either lives alone or shares an apartment with one or more people who are not relatives. Two

Table 2.8. Income Classes

	1950	1970
High Income		
families	$10,000 and over	$15,000 and over
individuals	$7,000 and over	$10,000 and over
Middle Income		
families	$5,000 to $10,000	$7,000 to $15,000
individuals	$3,500 to $7,000	$5,000 to $10,000
Lower Income		
families	$5,000 and under	$7,000 and under
individuals	$3,500 and under	$5,000 and under

INCOME DISTRIBUTION: 1950 CENSUS

	Families			Individuals			All Households	
Upper income	Over $10,000	98,905	5%	Over $7,000	15,815	3%	114,720	4%
Middle income	$5,000-$10,000	460,960	23%	$3,500-$7,000	70,185	11%	531,145	20%
Lower income	Under $5,000	1,437,150	72%	Under $3,500	569,445	87%	2,006,595	76%
		1,997,015	100%		655,445	100%	2,652,460	100%

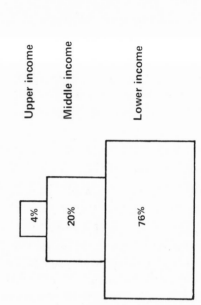

Upper income — 4%

Middle income — 20%

Lower income — 76%

roommates might have incomes totaling $17,000. However, because they are unrelated individuals, the Census counts them as separate households, with incomes of, say, $9,500 and $7,500. It is assumed here that an unrelated individual needs approximately two-thirds the income of a family to maintain membership in a comparable economic bracket.

The income distribution for 1950 found the great majority of New York's households clustered at the bottom of a low-slung economic pyramid. Close to 75 percent of the city's families reported incomes of less than $5,000, while more than 85 percent of its single persons earned under $3,500. In other words, most New Yorkers lived modestly, had little to lose, and—perhaps most important—realized that their own condition was shared by most of their fellow citizens. Less than a fourth of the city's households qualified for the middle- and upper-income ranges. As the findings for employment and education have already indicated, New York had a relatively small middle class and only a slender stratum at the luxury level. If the very shape of the pyramid connotes a certain stability, it was because most people with low incomes either accepted their status or entertained modest ambitions for themselves. Low-income households were not looked upon as a "problem" in that generation, nor were more fortunate families regarded with enmity or envy. Most New Yorkers kept to their neighborhoods and were generally quiescent as citizens. They made it a comparatively passive city, with not a few of its residents displaying the composure of their peasant and chattel ancestors.

Twenty years brought New York into a new era. The income statistics make it plain that by 1970 the city had far fewer poor people than in its past. The low-income group had declined to less than half of the city's households, giving it a distinct minority status. (Even including those the Census failed to reach would not make the poor a majority.) During the two decades the middle range almost doubled in size. Those in the top bracket expanded to five times their earlier dimension, from a hardly visible 4 percent to 20 percent of the population. The number of single individuals with large incomes rose more than eightfold, from 15,815 to 131,730.

Within the "high-income" range, 361,542 families and

INCOME DISTRIBUTION: 1970 CENSUS

	Families			Individuals			All Households	
Upper income	Over $15,000	485,424	24%	Over $10,000	131,730	12%	617,154	20%
Middle income	$7,000-$15,000	892,593	43%	$5,000-$10,000	290,126	29%	1,182,719	39%
Lower income	Under $7,000	680,926	33%	Under $5,000	564,710	57%	1,245,636	41%
		2,058,943	100%		986,566	100%	3,045,509	100%

Upper income 20%

Middle income 39%

Lower income 41%

33,267 individuals had incomes between $15,000 and $25,000; 99,641 families and 12,231 individuals were between $25,000 and $50,000; and 24,241 families and 3,662 individuals received over $50,000. Unfortunately this breakdown cannot be compared with comparable figures for 1950, as that Census placed everyone earning over $10,000 in a single, undifferentiated category.

Why, then, does the belief persist that New York's middle class has suffered a net loss during the postwar period? The Census figures show that in terms of upgraded incomes and occupations, residents who stayed in the city have more than replaced those who left for the suburbs. Part of the answer stems from the fact that many of the city's salesmen, teachers, and office workers are no longer white. Prejudices being what they are, individuals holding these positions are not regarded as being "really" middle class. (If white New Yorkers are asked to list some middle-class neighborhoods, few will think of naming St. Albans.) In addition New York's upper income groups now contain more young people, single persons, and couples who either don't have children or whose children no longer live at home. Thus when references are made to middle-class losses, they mean that the city has fewer conventional families consisting of two parents and school-age children. Finally, New York now has a much larger number of households that depend for their income on public assistance or less legal sources. The fact that this group has grown in size persuades many people that the middle class must necessarily be smaller. In fact, families on welfare have supplanted not the middle class but rather, earlier low-income households whose members worked in domestic service or other unskilled jobs that have declined in number or no longer exist.

The approaching parity of the low- and middle-income classes (41 percent versus 39 percent) has had a far-reaching effect on political and social relationships. Their near numerical equality makes the two strata more noticeable to one another, with consequent comparisons that veer towards the invidious. Those in the middle-income range see the distance they have traveled and wonder why others cannot make the same kind of effort on their own initiative. They now have a standing to lose and are well aware of how tenuous that footing can be. Those left at the bottom, for their part, acknowledge no qualitative difference between themselves and those who have managed to do better. Middle-level and large incomes no longer go to only a fraction of the city's households, but now belong to a majority, most of whose members cannot claim any special abilities or outstanding achievements. The fracturing of the old income structure has aroused resentment and anxiety which once lay dormant. New York has paid a price for moving toward economic equality.

Neither the Census nor any other official agency has figures on inherited wealth or property holdings. No one knows how much New Yorkers have in their banks or portfolios or how many of them qualify as being substantially well-to-do. However, some information may be derived from reports the Internal Revenue Service issued concerning tax returns of 1969, its most recent release with city-by-city statistics. Of the 3,189,688 returns filed in New York, 153,427 had adjusted gross incomes of $15,000 or more, of which at least part came from dividends. (There were another 203,343 households with incomes over $15,000 but which had no dividend income.) Total dividend income for this group came to $1,231,098,248, or an impressive $8,024 per family. In postal district 10022, covering Manhattan's East Side from 50th Street to 60th Street, the *average* household among those receiving dividend income reported $21,484 from that source. And that includes families which had only a few hundred dollars from stocks or similar sources.

Many suburbs have incomes far surpassing even the most fashionable sections of the city. The median income in Scarsdale is $33,886. In Long Island, Old Westbury's median stands at $34,513 and Kings Point's reaches $40,971. No identifiable district of New York approaches those levels, although some blocks may reach that high. Even so, the average Scarsdale family that had dividend income received $7,346 from that source, while the figure for Kings Point is $8,550, the first below, and the second only slightly ahead of, the average for the city, and both are well behind New York's most affluent areas. Suburban prosperity depends mainly on month-by-month earnings, while the city's well-to-do receive more of their income from inherited or accumulated wealth.

ORIGINS AND OPPORTUNITIES

Everyone knows that white skin usually signifies higher income, a better job, and more extended schooling. But only the Census provides information on the precise extent of ethnic differentiation. At the outset it should be stressed that the racial groups have very different age compositions. Two-thirds of the city's Puerto Ricans and almost 60 percent of its blacks are under 30.[1] The white population, on the other hand, is well into middle age. Whites make up less than 70 percent of the city, yet they account for almost 90 percent of residents over 65. While blacks and Puerto Ricans comprise almost a third of the total population, they supply only 11 percent of the people over 65. Therefore, even if all migrations were to come to a halt, New York would year by year move toward becoming a preponderantly black and Puerto Rican city, simply as the current cohort of youngsters enters adulthood.

For example, the 1970 Census revealed that for every 100 white women in the 35–44 age range (their final decade of childbearing), the city had 230 white children, while 100 black women of the same age were matched with 290 children, and 100 Puerto Rican women had 330. Similarly, among New York's women between the ages of 10 and 39 who are currently at or will reach childbearing age during the 1970s, 4 out of 10 are black or Puerto Rican. Among the city's children under 10, the adult population a generation from now, black and Puerto Rican youngsters constitute 48 percent of the total. Even if all racial groups suddenly stabilized their numbers at zero replacement, the city would still end up with a white minority by the end of this century.

Puerto Ricans, with 10 percent of the families, can claim only 2 percent of the units earning over $15,000. Blacks account for 2 out of 10 of the city's families but only 1 in 10 of those earning over $15,000. By the same token, 83 percent of Puerto Rican families and 70 percent of black families have incomes below $10,000, whereas only 43 percent of the white families fall in that category. (At its highest reaches, New York has 24,241 families with incomes over $50,000. Of these, 868 are black and 170 are Puerto Rican.)

Employment figures follow much the same pattern. White

residents comprise 75 percent of the labor force, yet they hold 90 percent of the managerial positions and 87 percent of the professional and technical jobs. Despite their depressed situation, a higher proportion of Puerto Ricans have managerial positions than blacks, chiefly because more than twice as many own their own businesses as do blacks. In fact, the proportion of Puerto Ricans who own their own retail establishments now exceeds whites by almost 15 percent.

As far as education is concerned, over half of the white population has completed high school, contrasted with 20 percent of the Puerto Ricans and 41 percent of the blacks. Only 3,525 adult Puerto Ricans had graduated from college by 1970, 1 for every 97 of their number, compared with 1 of every 24 blacks. At the same time, Puerto Ricans seem to have done better than blacks when occupations are set alongside schooling. The proportion of blacks with white-collar jobs (43 percent) comes close to the percentage completing high school (41 percent), yet 34 percent of employed Puerto Ricans have obtained white-collar positions despite only 20 percent of them having finished high school.

Notwithstanding claims of black progress in recent years, a mere 11 percent of the black families earn more than $15,000, compared with almost three times as many whites. It has been argued that only that many blacks have qualified themselves for higher-salaried positions. As it turns out, the Census suggests the reverse. While 11 percent of the city's black families have incomes exceeding $15,000, coincidentally, 11 percent of the city's black residents have also attended college. On the other hand, while 30 percent of the white families are above $15,000, only 21 percent of them went to college.

Quite obviously, white New Yorkers have obtained more than their statistical share of the higher incomes and preferred positions that the city has to offer. Part of this advantage comes from their being older and therefore available when early opportunities were distributed. If blacks and Puerto Ricans possessing the same aptitudes and abilities as whites find themselves with lower earnings and less agreeable occupations, the Census statistics show the degrees of discrimination. Were incomes and occupations distributed randomly and regardless of race, then 132,927 of the city's white families with incomes over $10,000 a year would have to learn to live at a lower standard, and 137,007 white persons would have to hand over their white-collar jobs to a black or Puerto Rican replacement.

Ethnicity also includes white persons who maintain an identity with their country of origin. As indicated earlier, New York has 2,778,534 residents who were themselves born abroad or one or both of whose parents were. The Census provides detailed information for the city's black and Puerto Rican citizens, but it has not produced similar material for white individuals of foreign extraction. The closest approximations lie in some information on foreign-stock persons in the entire metropolitan area but without separate statistics for the city itself. Those figures include somewhat over a million suburban residents, many of whom may not have the same characteristics as their city cousins. Still, it seems unlikely that the two groups are totally dissimilar, in which case a brief look at the Census' findings may be of value.

First- and second-generation New Yorkers are well into middle age, with almost two-thirds of them having passed their 45th birthdays. In most cases their parents came to this country in the wave of immigration that ended in 1914. Being an older group, their educational attainments tend to be modest. Only half of those of Irish, German, and Polish stock finished high school. The exception is the predominantly Jewish "Russian" group, of whom 62 percent completed high school and nearly a third attended college. Italian-Americans in the metropolitan area may be compared with another ethnic group:

Information on the "mother tongue," the language spoken in a person's home during his childhood, provides additional insight. Where the language was other than English, as it was in most homes, Yiddish predominated in the "Russian" and "Polish" households. Indeed, Russian itself was spoken in less than 10 percent of the families who came from that country, and only another 2 or 3 percent spoke Ukrainian. Similarly, New York has

	Italians		Blacks	
Attended college	79,963	9%	104,473	11%
Graduated from high school	223,153	26	283,954	30
Did not finish high school	547,534	64	570,441	59
	850,650	100%	958,868	100%

never had a large Polish settlement, in contrast to other urbanized areas. Only 31 percent of its Polish-stock homes used the
Polish language, contrasted with 71 percent in Cleveland, 77 in
Chicago, 80 in Detroit, and 85 in Buffalo. On the other hand,
more than two-thirds of the German stock households in New
York spoke German. Still, many of these may have been Jewish
homes, as German Jews did not speak Yiddish to nearly the
degree that their Russian and Polish counterparts did. Only 16
percent of the Italian-Americans reported that English was
spoken in their childhood homes, in contrast to 26 percent for
those of Russian stock, which suggests a more strenuous effort by
the latter to accept the manners of their new country. Finally,
the Census reports that 15 individuals of Irish ancestry in the
New York metropolitan area listed Ukrainian as their mother
tongue.

MANHATTAN IS DIFFERENT

Of course, Manhattan is different. More than half its
households consist of people living on their own, twice the proportion of any other borough. Over 12 percent of its households
had incomes exceeding $25,000 in 1970, nearly twice the propor-
tion in Queens, the second wealthiest borough. Manhattan contains most of the real wealth in New York. It has 14,085 families
with incomes over $50,000, more than all the other boroughs put
together. Its residents account for 80 percent of the entire city's
dividend income. Manhattan households averaged $7,600 from
that source in 1970, compared with $1,020 in the other boroughs.
One-fourth of its workers hold professional or related positions,
as against 15 percent for Queens, which ranks second in that area
of employment. And 21 percent of its adults have completed
college, compared with 10 percent in Queens and less than 7
percent in Brooklyn. More of its families own a second home, and
a higher proportion send their children to nursery schools.

Yet Manhattan contains large, low-income areas such as
Harlem and the Lower East Side, not to mention the rooming
houses and hotels of the Times Square area. A higher proportion
of its population is over 65 than in any other borough, and along
with the Bronx, it leads in families headed by a woman. Quite

obviously Manhattan is a mixture. It even has Inwood at its northern tip, a residential neighborhood which could be mistaken for parts of Brooklyn or Queens. Any statistical portrayal combines extremes in wealth and education, which means that its prosperous part is even better off than the overall figures suggest. Some of its elderly residents are very wealthy, and not a few of the women raising children on their own have professional jobs and middle-class incomes. The borough's "single" population includes not only stockbrokers and stewardesses but also the derelicts and addicts who congregate on its street corners.

Manhattan has been losing population at a steady rate, descending from 1,960,101 in 1950 to 1,539,225 in 1970, a drop of 21 percent. (Brooklyn, the other declining borough, went down by only 5 percent in this period.) Those leaving tended to be families with younger children, black as well as white. The loss would have been even more severe were it not for the arrival of newcomers. Manhattan stands well ahead of the other boroughs in its share of people who have recently moved in from another state. Some of these contribute little to the well-being of the city; urban centers have always attracted many of society's rejects and dropouts. But many have auspicious credentials. Between 1960 and 1970 Manhattan residents holding professional positions increased from 120,016 to 173,866, while those with college degrees went from 156,203 to 213,586. These are impressive advances for only 10 years, and at a time when the borough itself was losing numbers.

The question is not *whether* every Manhattan resident fits into a preconceived category, but *how many* do. Representing less than 20 percent of the population of New York, it contributes a disproportionate share of those people we associate with the cosmopolitan aspects of the city's life. Whether it has the preponderance of such individuals is difficult to say. For example, over half of the subscribers to *New York* magazine and the *Village Voice* live in Manhattan. On the other hand, the other boroughs combined buy more copies of the *New York Times*. Brooklyn, Queens, and the Bronx obviously have a liberal and literate middle class, notwithstanding that their members tend to display more conventional tastes and domestic preoccupations. More important, Manhattan has more of the sort of people who support the institutions and amenities that make Manhattan a world capital. Museums, galleries, and concert halls all depend on the patronage of these individuals, as do the deluxe restaurants, fashion houses, and interior designers who link New York to other international centers. The Census has no statistics to identify these tastes and talents, but it has enough hints to verify the suspicion that the urban life is made primarily by people who choose to live, as well as work, in the heart of the city.

CITY AND SUBURBS: GAINS AND LOSSES

People have been quitting the city for nearly a generation, with the suburbs their most common destination, and these departures have been mainly white families with above-average incomes. Yet, despite these desertions, city residents have continued to hold their own in terms of higher education, professional occupations, and comfortable earnings. It may be of some value, therefore, to look more deeply into who has been leaving the city and what sorts of people have been taking their place. The traditional stereotypes simply do not hold.

The Census asks everyone where they lived five years earlier. From these responses it factors out information on those persons who moved from New York to the suburbs between 1965 and 1970 and the same for people who moved into the city. But one or two warnings are needed here. First, the information deals only with movements during the five-year period. Figures are not available for migrations between 1960 and 1964, although the 1960 Census has its set of statistics for movements from 1955 to 1960. It is a bit like trying to picture someone you can see only from the waist up. Second, the "suburbs" covered are Westchester, Rockland, Nassau, and Suffolk counties in New York State, thus excluding any New York City residents who moved to suburban New Jersey or Connecticut. As a result, the Census understates the extent of the out-migration. Nevertheless, the percentage distributions given are probably fairly representative. There is no reason to believe that people who moved to Bergen county in New Jersey have a social profile much different from those who chose Westchester or Long Island.

Between 1965 and 1970 a total of 283,007 persons moved into the city and 342,941 departed for its suburbs, making a net

Table 2.11. Mobility in Metropolitan Area, 1965–70

	Moved into New York City		Moved to Suburbs from New York City		Moved to Suburbs from Elsewhere	
Age						
5 to 19	49,344	17%	109,522	32%	45,885	31%
20 to 29	140,880	50	61,255	18	44,892	30
30 to 44	50,029	18	100,287	29	33,365	23
45 to 64	31,258	11	46,974	14	15,625	11
65 and over	11,496	4	24,903	7	6,919	5
total	283,007	100%	342,941	100%	146,686	100%
Education						
4+ years of college	61,142	39%	44,458	21%	33,108	41%
1 to 3 years of college	23,425	15	28,513	13	12,680	16
completed high school	36,813	23	76,030	35	20,744	26
less than high school	35,431	23	65,711	31	13,668	17
Total	156,811	100%	214,712	100%	80,200	100%
Occupations (men)						
professional and technical	32,591	36%	23,089	23%	17,037	40%
managers and administrators	12,560	14	16,876	17	8,408	20
clerical and sales	21,012	24	19,135	20	7,297	17
nonwhite collar	23,835	26	39,362	40	10,305	24
Total	89,998	100%	98,462	100%	43,047	100%

loss of 59,934. As might be expected, children and their parents accounted for most of these departures. Only 6 percent of those who left the city were single. In contrast, half of the 283,007 newcomers to New York were in their twenties, and 40 percent of the adult arrivals were unmarried. The city's loss of 59,934 persons just about equals the 60,178 children who were taken away during this period. Put another way, more adults—admittedly, only 244—actually moved into New York than departed for the four outlying counties covered by the Census.

The Census offers information on employment for men only. Those figures show that more men with professional occupations moved into New York than left. In fact, 36 percent of the arrivals held such jobs, compared with only 23 percent of the departures. The largest single group among those leaving were blue-collar workers. The pattern with regard to education was similar. A markedly higher proportion of arrivals to the city had completed college (39 percent), compared with individuals who moved out (21 percent). Among those going to the suburbs, two-thirds had only a high school diploma, a status shared by less than half of the city's newcomers. All in all, the people who migrated from New York to its suburbs were not a particularly elite segment of the citizenry. Most belonged to the clerical or blue-collar classes.

The Census uses a very odd method for comparing incomes in its migration tables. It aggregates in a single column the number of "persons in families with family incomes" of particular amounts. Thus, for example, its tabulations appear to show that 39,297 out-migrants from the city had incomes exceeding $25,000. However, those 39,297 include everyone in the departing families: Tommy (age 6), Sarah (age 9), and Peter (age 14). By the same token, the Census reports only 20,226 in-migrants earning over $25,000. But more of those are husband-wife couples, with fewer children to swell the total. (Even with this bias, the tables still show that more than half the "individuals" moving to the suburbs belonged to families with incomes under $15,000.) To repeat, this is a most curious statistical method, and one used nowhere else in the Census.

Another set of statistics—newspaper circulation—tends to substantiate this interpretation. In 1949 the city's two morning tabloids, the *News* and the *Mirror,* had combined weekday circulations within the city averaging 2,243,900. In 1973 the one remaining tabloid, the *News*, sold 1,243,077 copies inside the city on a typical morning. This drop of 1,000,823, or 45 percent, reflects the number of working-class and lower-middle-class families who left the city during that period. The *Times* and the *Herald-Tribune* sold a total of 456,271 copies in 1949. In 1973 the *Times*, by itself, circulated 360,370 copies in the city, making a drop in readership of 95,901, or 21 percent. In actual numbers, New York's tabloid constituency suffered a tenfold decline compared with the class preferring a quality newspaper.

Interestingly, people who moved to the suburbs from outside the New York metropolitan area showed much more of the profile customarily associated with suburban life. In terms of schooling, occupation, and income, those who journeyed from a distance stood substantially higher on the social scale, compared with their neighbors who came out from the city. New York's economic and educational contributions to the suburbs are not terribly impressive when set alongside the attributes of those arriving from elsewhere in the country. The more affluent side of the suburbs depends chiefly on people moving in from Shaker Heights and Bloomfield Hills, rather than Crown Heights and Forest Hills.

A comparison of mobility, 1955–60 with 1965–70, shows a qualitative shift. In the earlier period 22,350 professional people entered New York, while 24,906 left, leaving a deficit of 2,556. Similarly, 44,198 college graduates moved into the city and 42,164 moved out, making a gain of only 2,034. However, Table 2.11 shows the more recent half decade gave the city a net gain of 9,502 professional people and 16,684 college graduates. Movement to the suburbs may continue, but it has lost its acceleration among the more highly educated. All in all, the flight to the outer fringe requires new analysis. Available figures suggest that the people leaving the city are not those who usually come to mind when the suburban explosion is cited. Furthermore, many of those departing have been replaced by individuals with traits and talents New York needs to retain its stature as a place of excitement and innovation.

3

The City's Politics

Between 1965 and 1973 New Yorkers cast more than 20 million ballots in successive elections. It stands to reason that patterns can be found, trends uncovered, and ideologies identified in these figures. Most citizens take the trouble to vote because they believe that at least one of the candidates is engaged in something more than trying to get a government job. They see their vote as advancing a program, even a philosophy. Personal hopes and fears, combined with conceptions of the public good which have been many years in forming, find expression on election day. Twenty million such decisions should produce some data for characterizing a body politic.

Even so, deducing values from the way people vote can be dangerous. After all, a ballot simply signifies a preference for one candidate—or often a dislike for another. The more elaborate the analysis, the less it can rest on evidence. Different people may support a single party, person, or program, for the most varied of motives. Nor can one impose an extrinsic logic on another person's politics. In one year a citizen may mark his ballot for Smith, yet in the following election he will vote for Jones who opposes Smith on every issue. Voters create their own consistencies. They refuse to pattern their politics for the convenience of others. Some ballots express economic class, ethnic origins, or other visible attributes. With other individuals such traits bear no relation to their electoral preferences. Of course, votes have meaning; why else make the trip to the polls? Of course, voters have

48

reasons; few select their lever by tossing a coin. Yet meanings and reasons do not lie "within" the figures. Politics is not so sufficiently formulated a science as to provide its own explanations. Accordingly, responsibility for the interpretations in this book rests with me.

THE PARTIES

Politicians and platforms come and go, but party affiliations have remained surprisingly constant in the city.

While the Republican figure declined by 15,507, the combined Republican–Conservative enrollment rose sufficiently to keep that side of the spectrum at 20 percent of the citywide total. Similarly, Democratic and Liberal registrations stayed at 72 percent. The two third parties together made gains of 83,113, suggesting a modest advance in the number of ideologically inclined voters. That rise was more than offset by 102,630 new registrants who gave no party listing. At first glance the 283,458 increase in overall registrations suggests a growth in political interest over the eight-year period. What actually occurred was that getting on the books became much easier, due to the ending of literacy tests and some concerted campaigns to sign up people in their own neighborhoods or on major thoroughfares. However, the election returns suggest that few of the newly signed citizens ever went to the polls. In the 1964 presidential contest, for example, 91 percent of those on the registration rolls turned out to vote; in 1972 only 72 percent made the effort. Even more strikingly, in 1965, 77 percent of the 3,281,689 registered voters took part in the

Table 3.1. Political Party Affiliations, 1965 and 1973

	1965		1973	
Republicans	662,146	20%	646,639	18%
Democrats	2,318,478	71	2,431,700	68
Conservatives	15,565	—	65,387	2
Liberals	61,870	2	95,161	3
No party	223,630	7	326,260	9
	3,281,689	100%	3,565,147	100%

mayoral race. In 1973 a mere 47 percent of the 3,565,147 participated. The whole question of declining turnouts deserves more discussion. If the political process—or the candidates it puts forward—appeals to less than half the population, then conventional ideas about the capacities and constituencies of government need reexamination.

Only a minority of the city's voters can be regarded as party regulars. The sternest test of Democratic loyalty came in 1969 when the party found itself with Mario Procaccino as its candidate for mayor. He received only 831,772 votes, a figure equal to 40 percent of that year's Democratic registrations. On the other side, in 1973 John Marchi managed to rally 275,362 Republican stalwarts, representing 43 percent of his party's registrants. Using still another test, party commitments sink even lower. In 1969, 221,064 Republicans and 777,796 Democrats participated in their party's mayoral primary, in both cases only 37 percent of those listed on their rolls. Party simply doesn't mean very much to most New York voters.

Candidates running on the Democratic, Republican, and Liberal lines have all got more than a million votes at one time or another. These showings, however, obviously do not reflect the followings of the parties, but rather the popularity of the candidates using their space. Similarly, while James Buckley, the Conservative candidate for the Senate in 1970, received 791,150 votes, a surer measure of that party's intrinsic appeal may be found in the 109,833 votes its own gubernatorial candidate got that same year when running against Nelson Rockefeller. By the same token, the Liberals' showing dipped to 109,462 when the Liberal party was used as an alternative way of supporting George McGovern in 1972. Putting these statistics together, it emerges that about 1.3 million New Yorkers, or 37 percent of all those registered, can be called "party" voters. From among the remaining 63 percent (only half of whom usually turn out to vote) come citywide margins of victory.

Prior to the 1974 gubernatorial landslide, only two candidates had won a majority on a single party's line: Hubert Humphrey in 1968 and Abraham Beame in 1973. George McGovern achieved a majority inside the city but only by using two designations.[1] Everyone else who came in first did so with a plurality.

The typical city election has three candidates, and the typical winner finishes with about 46 percent of the vote. Only occasionally will a party get a majority, including the Democrats, despite their having 68 percent of the registrations.

New York's Republicans deserve separate study. That as many as 646,639 people register with that party may come as a surprise, considering how seldom they reach public notice (Manhattan's 515,731 registered Democrats get several times as much attention). Even in 1964, at the lowest ebb of Republican fortunes, the city gave Barry Goldwater 801,877 votes, or more than he got in Montana, Kansas, and Nebraska together. As it happens, Manhattan has less than 20 percent of the Republican registrations. The old Silk Stocking district of the Upper East Side is now a Democratic domain. If it still supports some Republicans, it demands that they display liberal credentials. The real Republican strongholds are in Bay Ridge and Bath Beach in Brooklyn, in Ridgewood and Sunnyside in Queens, in Schuylerville in the northern Bronx, plus long stretches of Staten Island. The form of Republicanism encountered in these areas has much in common with its Syracuse and Indianapolis counterparts.

Candidates such as Jacob Javits and Charles Goodell can expect to lose the votes of several hundred thousand Republican regulars. Javits' 1968 victory came from people who customarily support the Democrats' candidates. About 40 percent of those who consider themselves Republicans prefer to record their ballots on the Conservative line. For example, in his 1969 race for mayor, John Marchi got only 329,506 Republican votes, a mere 14 percent of the poll. It took another 212,905 votes in the Conservative column to save him from total humiliation. Running again as a Republican, but this time without the Conservative endorsement, Marchi's 1973 showing dropped to 275,362 votes. A substantial plurality of Republicans uses the Conservative option to demonstrate their ideological independence. These defections reflect a quiet struggle within the city's conservative classes between the older and more established and the newly arrived echelons of the middle class. Someone who owns his own insurance agency on Fort Hamilton Parkway will probably tend to vote the Republican line consistently. On the other hand, a construction worker in Woodhaven will as often as not go along with the Conservative endorsement. This revolt against the gentry first showed itself in 1961 when Lawrence Gerosa, running on a "citizens" ticket against Louis Lefkowitz and Robert Wagner, received 321,604 votes. William Buckley, running in 1965 and receiving 341,226 votes, was continuing a conservative consciousness Gerosa had already awakened four years earlier.

CIVILIAN REVIEW AND ITS CONSEQUENCES

Until fairly recently campaign issues in the city were the traditional ones—corruption, machine politics, economy in government. Fiorello LaGuardia won in 1933 because too many Democrats had become too visibly dishonest. In 1950 Vincent Impellitteri led the field on his own "experience" ticket by persuading enough people that he was the only candidate not beholden to the bosses. Most of the time the ballot contained forgettable names such as Harold Riegelman, Jonah Goldstein, Edward Corsi, and Robert Christenberry, none of whom took distinguishable positions on the governance of the city.

Even in the 1965 election in which John Lindsay became mayor, campaigning following the traditional pattern. Lindsay said little that was taken as controversial, nor did he give much hint about the administrative posture he would adopt. As a result he attracted votes from two dissimilar constituencies. On one side, he ran well among mid-Manhattan Democrats who had followed his record as a liberal congressman. In the assembly districts reaching from 14th Street to Harlem, his majorities ranged from 63 to 78 percent. Those voters were sufficiently familiar with his Washington record and personal style to sense the kind of mayor he would be. On the other side, Lindsay won majorities in places such as Bay Ridge and Fort Hamilton in Brooklyn, and Hollis and Douglaston in Queens. These were traditional Republican territory where voters supported him simply because he was their party's nominee. Their Republican fealties were so unquestioning that they ignored William Buckley, the Conservative candidate, and rallied behind a man about whom they knew little other than that he was running on Row A.

Only after the voting machines were back in the warehouse did New York begin to gain the measure of John Lindsay. Virtually his first, and certainly his most symbolic, act was to create a civilian review board to entertain charges of brutal or insulting behavior by the police. The panel, composed of three police officers and four civilians, was set up chiefly for black and Hispanic citizens who had become increasingly vocal in their complaints about the police. Such tribunals had been established elsewhere, notably Rochester and Philadelphia. Their very conduct turned the role and conduct of the police into a political issue. In New York, abetted by expensive propaganda campaigns, citizens found themselves forced to take sides: were you a supporter or an opponent of the police department?

As matters emerged, a middle ground on this question became impossible. The Patrolmen's Benevolent Association distributed petitions and got enough signatures to place abolition of the Civilian Review Board on the November 1966 ballot. Voters were asked to amend the city charter to require that any review agency be wholly police-staffed. The referendum soon turned into a catalyst for a more general discomfort that was spreading throughout the city. It provided what amounted to an opportunity for a vote of confidence on John Lindsay's first 10 months in office, but more important, it brought to the surface some issues which had hitherto been considered off limits in election campaigns.

Arguing the proposition simply on its merits, a Yes vote expressed the view that a review board with a majority of independent members would impede police performance. A No vote expressed the view that to keep a check on police practices was just as important, even if such scrutiny made the ordinary patrolman's job more difficult. Of the New Yorkers who entered the polling booths on November 8, 1966 (an election for governor was also occurring that day), 2,078,501 lifted their hands to the top of the machine and pulled one of the levers. The result showed substantial support for the police:

Yes (abolish the board)   1,313,201   63%
No (maintain the board)   765,300   37%

The importance of the referendum lay in the fact that it aligned the electorate according to sentiments which had previously been barred from politics. Before 1966 candidates had sidestepped uncomfortable questions, while referendums dealt with innocuous statewide amendments. But once civilian review of the police reached the ballot, it made visible a division that would affect almost all later elections. Feelings shown in that vote would appear again in races ranging from presidential elections down to mayoral primaries.

Most people explained their Yes ballots in terms of the rising incidence of crime. It goes without saying that more New Yorkers live in fear of burglary, robbery, and assault than at any time in living memory. Even locked doors and lighted streets no longer provide assurance against the eventuality of attack. Of all the services sought by citizens, safety obviously heads the list. Accordingly, the argument against the review board carried force. It was claimed that officers would hesitate in their duties, wondering whether their actions might lead to retribution by a tribunal unable to appreciate on-the-spot decisions. Many New Yorkers (obviously most of those voting) were reluctant to take a gamble that might weaken what they already regarded as inadequate protection. With fear of crime rampant, the inclination to give the police the benefit of the doubt swayed about two-thirds of the voters to the Yes position.

Several scholars have stressed this line of reasoning. One study asserted that "New York's residential patterns are such that nearly every remaining sanctuary of law and order abuts a high-crime area, representing a threat to personal safety." Of course, no neighborhood in the city is completely immune from the violence originating in lower-class areas. At the same time, the city has many residential sections that are still considerably distant from the nearest slum, and most of these have comparatively low crime rates. The typical householder may well regard one nearby holdup as one too many. Even so, the amount of support for the police in low-crime areas begins to suggest that people had more on their minds than simply making their own streets safer. For example, 73 percent of the voters in Brooklyn's Bensonhurst sided with the police even though their rate of reported robberies was only 14 per 10,000 residents. Borough Park in Brooklyn went 85 percent against the Civilian Review Board despite an identical

him. In Bay Ridge and Fort Hamilton, Lindsay won 52 percent of the votes in 1965; by 1969 his share there had slipped to a mere 18 percent. He had to make up for these losses if he was to improve on his referendum showing.

The accepted explanation for Lindsay's victory was summed up on a *New York Times'* election headline: "Poor and Rich, Not Middle-Class, the key to Lindsay Re-Election. Mayor Lindsay won re-election with an unusual combination of support from higher-income New Yorkers and low-income Negroes and Puerto Ricans. Large segments of middle-income groups voted against his continuing in power." While this depiction of the voting has a plausible ring, it also carries some misplaced emphases. To begin with, the mayor's total contained very few "low income" voters and perhaps none at all. Moreover, his black and Latin backers comprised only a very minor part of his following. There is good reason to believe that he could have won reelection even had every black and Spanish-speaking voter remained at home that day. One source of evidence, a CBS election-day poll, revealed that had the electorate somehow been limited to only white voters, Lindsay still would have run ahead of his opponents.

Lindsay's showing in the city's dozen predominantly black and Hispanic assembly districts came to less than his margin over Procaccino, his closest contender. In other words, he would have won reelection even if all the votes from Harlem, Bedford-Stuyvesant, Brownsville, South Jamaica, and the South Bronx had been removed from the citywide totals. The appearance of strong support arose from high percentages but exceedingly low turnouts. Receiving 76 percent of the votes in Brownsville looked impressive until it emerged that only 13,377 people had voted there. Lindsay would appear to have done much more poorly in Little Neck where his share was 32 percent, yet because the turnout in Little Neck was 49,925, his 32 percent there brought him more actual votes than his 76 percent in Brownsville.

While it was true that many middle-income New Yorkers voted against Lindsay, the fact remains that what returned him to City Hall were votes from New Yorkers who had opposed the Civilian Review Board but who were won over to him during his reelection campaign. Most of these conversions occurred in middle-class neighborhoods throughout the city.

The best way to analyze this achievement comes from a direct comparison of the 1966 and 1969 returns. Lindsay surpassed the No vote on abolishing civilian review by 247,333, the difference between 1,012,633 and 765,300. In contrast, Procaccino and Marchi together only exceeded the Yes vote by 60,982, the difference between 1,374,183 and 1,313,201. Thus Lindsay's "net increase" from 1966 to 1968 came to 186,351 votes—the difference between his gross increase of 247,333 and the Procaccino–Marchi increase of 60,982. The way to discover how Lindsay created a constituency is by ascertaining which segments of the city contributed most largely to his net gain of 186,351, for every such shift represented a New Yorker who switched from supporting the police to supporting the mayor. (As it happened, the net-gain figure of 186,351 approximated Lindsay's 180,861 plurality over Procaccino. However, this similarity is mainly a statistical coincidence.)

In every borough except Staten Island, Lindsay's increase over the No vote of 1966 exceeded the Procaccino–Marchi margin over the Yes vote for abolishing civilian review. In the Bronx the mayor's two opponents gained only 7,585 votes over the antireview board total, and in Queens their gain came to only 8,871. At the same time, Lindsay's net gains in Brooklyn and the Bronx were relatively modest. If they are combined with his Staten Island loss, he was still only 35,885 votes ahead of civilian review in those three boroughs that included half of the city's electorate. His most substantial inroads, which won him reelection, were in Manhattan and Queens which together contributed more than 80 percent of his net gain between 1966 and 1969.

Traditionally Manhattan is the most liberal of the five boroughs, contributing a higher proportion of its votes to progressive causes and candidates. So it came as no surprise that more than half of Lindsay's new votes came from Manhattan. Out of his citywide gain of 186,351, no fewer than 102,098 ballots were produced in the central borough. But it should be noted that the assembly districts comprising Harlem and East Harlem surpassed their referendum showing by only modest amounts, once more suggesting that black and Hispanic voters gave important but not crucial support to the Lindsay campaign. The real—indeed, quite extraordinary—increases came from the white neighborhoods surrounding Central Park. Three East Side assembly districts, running from 14th to 96th Streets, produced 43,127 new Lindsay votes, or almost a quarter of his entire citywide gain. Those additional votes could not be attributed to population growth. Despite the boom in residential construction on the East Side during the 1960s, the electoral participation rate in its assembly districts rose less between 1966 and 1969 than it did in the city as a whole.

Votes from Manhattan's East and West Sides were the major instruments of Lindsay's reelection. His net gain in their assembly districts outdistanced the advances he made in all of Brooklyn and Queens taken together. His opponents were correct in characterizing the mayor's chief constituency as a "Manhattan arrangement." But what needs emphasizing is that this source of support had been created virtually within a three-year period. If Lindsay had to rely on his referendum supporters, his slim Manhattan majority there would have been insufficient to offset his opponents' strength elsewhere in the city.

Lindsay's gain of 48,423 votes in Queens was of secondary importance in his reelection. The conventional assumption was that he had managed to win back Jewish voters who had become disaffected during the 1968 Ocean Hill–Brownsville school dispute and the teachers' strike that followed. But the returns in Queens showed that it was no longer possible to generalize about a "Jewish vote." Many older Jews, especially in Brooklyn, tended to identify with the teachers and refused to support Lindsay. However, in parts of Queens, as in Manhattan, a younger Jewish constituency was emerging, one that had no special sympathy with the teachers or their union. Lindsay scored a net gain of 4,344 votes in the Forest Hills assembly district; he also did well in the Rego Park area where he bettered his referendum figure by 3,424. Referring to these voters by their religion is not very helpful. In fact, they belong to a new stratum where ethnic origins have little influence on electoral behavior.

Lindsay made more gains in the Ozone Park and Woodhaven assembly district, a largely Catholic section of Queens. In an area where 82 percent of the voters had opposed the review board, the mayor augmented his 1966 total by 5,041 votes. In Sunnyside and Maspeth, also predominantly Catholic and which went 81 percent against civilian review, he gained 4,187 votes. Put very simply, the city had a lot of Catholic residents who preferred a Protestant Lindsay to a Catholic Marchi or Procaccino. The CBS survey mentioned above found that over a quarter of the city's Catholics voted for Lindsay's reelection and that a third of his total vote was cast by Catholics. This meant that Catholics contributed only about 10,000 fewer votes for him than did Jews. The figures suggest that younger and better-educated Catholics, particularly in Queens, had developed values compatible with the Lindsay candidacy. Apparently their own ethnicity had little effect on their voting decision. The willingness of people in Woodhaven, Sunnyside, and Maspeth to support someone who was not only a Social Register Episcopalian and Vietnam dove but a politician who spent more time in Harlem than in their own neighborhoods should make it evident that there had come into being a political constituency which could no longer be explained by conventional categories of ethnic origins and residential location.

AN ATTENUATING ELECTORATE

The Democratic party had, for all intents and purposes, appropriated the 1973 election even before Lindsay announced that he would retire at the end of his second term. His 1969 victory on the Liberal line was a onetime occurrence. New York's politics had to return to their rightful owners—the party that boasted nearly 70 percent of the voters. One consequence of this preponderance of numbers is a long list of contestants for the party's nominations. In 1969 five people had entered themselves for the mayoral candidacy, with three of them dividing 90 percent of the poll in almost equal proportions. Procaccino received 33 percent of the votes, Robert Wagner got 29 percent, and Herman Badillo finished with 28 percent. Accordingly, the party had to run Procaccino despite his poor campaigning style, conservative politics, and inauspicious plurality. Norman Mailer also took part in that primary, but his renown in other quarters did not carry over into politics, and he came away with only 41,288 votes. There is the possibility that Badillo might have won the primary had Mailer not run. Badillo ended up only 38,364 votes behind Procaccino, and it seems likely that almost all of Mailer's backers would have supported Badillo if the novelist had withdrawn. Democratic primaries tend to be fratricidal. Even the most naive voter can see the interplay of personal ambitions. Each aspirant believes that he and only he can do justice to the position. No one ever steps down or aside to help anyone else, even if such obduracy jeopardizes their common approach to politics. Egos engaged themselves in a similar manner in 1973.

A Republican-dominated state legislature, seeing an opportunity to institutionalize Democratic factionalism, ruled that if the frontrunner in a party primary did not get at least 40 percent of the votes, the top two contenders would have to face one another in a runoff. The 1973 primary had four entrants, making up an ideological array not unlike the field four years earlier. Mario Biaggi replaced Mario Procaccino on the conservative side. Abraham Beame took Robert Wagner's and James Scheuer's places in the center. And, as before, two liberals insisted on entering. Herman Badillo ran again, and Albert Blumenthal, in a manner of speaking, took Norman Mailer's place. Compared with 1969, primary sentiment seemed to have shifted slightly to the left.

The runoff primary between Beame and Badillo offered some indication of how far the Bronx congressman could expand his following. That confrontation, held four weeks later, showed that the issues from the 1966 referendum still held sway in city

Table 3.2.

1969			1973		
(Total vote: 777,796)			(Total vote: 772,699)		
Procaccino	33%		Biaggi	21%	
Wagner	29				
Scheuer	5	(34%)	Beame	34	
Badillo	28				
		(33%)	Badillo	29	(45%)
Mailer	5		Blumenthal	16	
	100%			100%	

politics. Badillo may have been a lawyer and accountant, a resident of Riverdale, and six feet tall, but he was also a Puerto Rican.

It seems a safe estimate that at least half of Badillo's ballots in the first 1973 primary came from white voters. In the six virtually all-white assembly districts of mid-Manhattan, he received more votes than Blumenthal. Liberal white areas in Brooklyn and Queens, which had rallied for Lindsay's reelection, also contributed substantially to Badillo's total. He did well in black and Hispanic neighborhoods. The issue was whether he could become a citywide candidate able to draw votes from a range of races and classes. In this respect Badillo would have to show some similarity to Thomas Bradley of Los Angeles or Coleman Young of Detroit, both of whom did well enough in white districts to defeat white opponents. With Biaggi and Blumenthal out of the primaries, Badillo appeared to have a fighting chance for the nomination—but that assumption overlooked the legacy of 1966.

Only 772,699 Democrats participated in the first primary, less than a third of those eligible and even fewer than the 1969 figure. The widely held view was that Beame was a sure winner, even with a light turnout, so people stayed home. Hence the consternation in many quarters when Badillo finished within 42,626 votes of Beame's total, plus the fact that the combined Badillo–Blumenthal total surpassed Beame's by a margin of 80,615 votes. At that point people began to see Badillo not as a legitimate, citywide candidate but as a spokesman for the black and Spanish-speaking segments of the city. Many white voters will support a black or Hispanic candidate if he or she appears to have muted racial attachments. Carl Stokes, Thomas Bradley, Coleman Young, and other mayoral winners betokened middle-class values and did not seem to symbolize the anger or hostility endemic in so much of race relations. In a word, they were not perceived as mayors white voters had to fear. Their election was not construed as a sign that blacks would take greater liberties within the city.

The prospect of a Badillo victory was taken just this way in many circles. Were he to become mayor, people persuaded themselves, new and less-than-subtle signs of arrogance would soon show themselves in the streets, schools, and elsewhere. The issue was not Herman Badillo as mayor but rather how his election might arouse his supporters. After all, the Civilian Review Board referendum was supposed to have settled that question.

What happened, simply, was that 129,644 additional Democrats turned out for the second primary. Beame's share in that runoff more than doubled, rising from 266,462 votes to 548,532, or from 34 to 61 percent of the total. In contrast, Badillo's showing rose only from 223,836 to 353,811. It seems safe to assume that both Beame and Badillo made every effort to unearth supporters who failed to vote in the first primary. In that respect, Beame voters were easier to find, whereas Badillo had come much closer to exhausting his electorate in the initial balloting. In the average assembly district where Badillo held the lead in the first primary, only 1,832 new voters turned up for the runoff. Among the assembly districts where Beame ran ahead in the first vote, 2,550 additional voters came out for the second balloting. In the Bronx, Badillo's home borough, the districts where he had first run ahead drew 2,251 new voters in the second round. In Beame's home borough, Brooklyn, districts he won in the first primary averaged 3,452 further voters in the runoff.

In Manhattan, Badillo's total rose predictably from 73,676 votes at first to 112,786 in the runoff, which came to about the same thing as inheriting all of Blumenthal's ballots. The only trouble was that Manhattan's turnout only rose by 6 percent, whereas in Brooklyn, where Beame did best, participation expanded by 26 percent. In three of Manhattan's assembly districts the numbers voting actually fell from the first to the second primary, even while the citywide turnout rose by 129,644 votes. These happened to be Blumenthal strongholds, suggesting no great effort on their part to find votes for Badillo. One of these districts, circling midtown from Yorkville to Central Park West, came up with only 6,540 votes for Badillo, compared with the 8,357 total it gave Badillo and Blumenthal in the opening primary. Yet this district managed to bring out 29,955 votes for George McGovern the year before. In other words, Badillo failed to find new support, not simply in the South Bronx and Bedford–Stuyvesant but also in Greenwich Village and Chelsea and along West End Avenue and Riverside Drive. It appears that even in Manhattan, Badillo could not advance further than the most liberal segment of the white electorate.

The second primary also showed the great difficulty of draw-ing black and Latin voters into the city's political processes. In a typical Badillo district, the Morrisania area of the Bronx, only 7,927 people voted in the runoff. Up in Co-op City, Beame country in the same borough, 33,082 people took part. In three Badillo districts in Brooklyn, encompassing Brownsville and Bed-ford–Stuyvesant, the total turnout was 19,054. The three Brook-lyn districts where Beame did best brought 72,050 people to the polls. The fact is that the majority of black and Spanish-speaking citizens remain outside the political pale. Even a strong candidate failed to attract voters other than those already accustomed to participating in elections.

Abraham Beame won the 1973 election with 57 percent of the votes, with his three opponents sharing the other 43 percent. John Marchi, the Republican again, and Mario Biaggi, the Con-servative, together drew 27 percent of the votes, compared with the 23 percent Marchi had achieved with the combined tickets in 1969. Albert Blumenthal, running as a Liberal, got 16 percent, hardly a repetition of Lindsay's 42 percent performance four years earlier. Considering that all of the contenders except Mar-chi were Democrats, candidates coming from that party got 74 percent of the votes.

The most important aspect of the election lay in another statistic, though. Only 1,683,489 people bothered to vote, which was an all-time low for New York City politics. This figure amounted to merely 52 percent of the city's 3,238,887 registered voters and a paltry 31 percent of its 5,358,207 residents eligible for the polls. (In other words, only 60 percent of all eligible citizens have registered.) For every three New Yorkers who voted, seven did not. Civics courses usually attribute lack of participation to apathy, in effect, laying the blame on the non-voter. It can also be argued that the decision to refrain from voting is both conscious and rational, that it is an informed political act. In these terms, 1973 may well have witnessed a widespread electoral boycott, the first such protest in the city's history.

Just a year before, 2,600,408 people had come out for the presidential election. In that contest both candidates were white, and the Democrat's record carried no special appeal for black and

Latin voters. Of course, there is always less participation in local races. But in 1969 only 204,806 fewer people voted than in 1968, whereas the drop from 1972 to 1973 came to 916,919, or more than four times as much. It is not sufficient to say that people remained home because a Beame victory seemed foreordained, for nonvoting varied considerably throughout the city.

In New York as a whole, turnout dipped by 35 percent between 1972 and 1973. Among the assembly districts where Beame led the field in the first primary, the drop in participation averaged 32 percent. In districts where Badillo had run ahead, 44 percent fewer people voted in 1973 than in 1972. As is well known, many of Badillo's supporters sat out the contest because their man was no longer a contender and they could not accept Blumenthal as a substitute. Even so, some districts displayed so sharp a fall in voting as to evoke additional explanation. In districts covering Brownsville and Bedford–Stuyvesant, for example, the turnout was about half that of 1972. In the Morrisiana and Hunts Point districts, less than 9,000 people voted for mayor, or less than half the number who showed up for the Nixon–McGovern race. Even Harlem, traditionally well-organized election territory, had declines from 45 to 47 percent. While various black and Latin officials eventually endorsed Beame, or in at least one case, Blumenthal, this encouragement went unheeded. Hunts Point actually recorded fewer votes in the November balloting than it had in the runoff primary. Word got around that the 1973 election would be one where white, and mainly middle-class, citizens would vie among themselves on issues holding no real interest for New Yorkers of other classes or colors. Who would win from among Beame, Biaggi, Blumenthal, and Marchi did not make any difference to 70 percent of the city's adult residents.

In 1972, the best among recent years for political participation, only 46 percent of New York's residents took the trouble to vote. In Nassau county 74 percent did, and in Westchester, 83 percent. Suburban citizens have higher incomes and educational levels, which are the major correlates with increased voting. Yet up in Hamilton County in the Adirondacks, no fewer than 82 percent of the potential electorate went to the polls. (In 1970, Hamilton County had a median family income of $7,019, the lowest in the state and well under New York City's $9,673.) The difference is that in upstate counties the political process has direct points of contact with everyday aspirations, even among the poor, which had once been the case in New York City as well.

Back in the 1952 presidential election, 3,411,473 New Yorkers went to the polls, almost one-third more than in 1972. Such participation meant that voting was much more widespread among lower-income citizens. The city's higher-income ranges accounted for only about a quarter of the city's households, so at least half of the active electorate had to consist of people with lower incomes who were prepared to identify with and participate in the city's politics. This involvement stemmed not from patronage, vote-buying, favors of local leaders, or the ethnic flavorings of the machines. There was simply the conviction that the victory of a particular candidate or party would directly affect one's own life and fortunes. This conviction is now missing for a majority of New Yorkers.

So many citizens now see casting a vote as being virtually irrelevant to their lives. Being governed by a Richard Nixon or a George McGovern, a Nelson Rockefeller or an Arthur Goldberg, a Marchi, a Biaggi, or Beame makes no difference to the character and quality of their existence. The responsibility lies mainly with a political system that does not have the resources to deal with conditions facing low-income citizens today. If New Yorkers display more indifference to elections than they did a generation ago, this is because the problems they face have outrun the capacity of politics to devise remedies. Actually the system's capabilities have not diminished over the decades. What have expanded are the kinds of conditions people find distasteful. They have no hope or expectation that government can cope with their grievances. Elections have become an arena where those in the middle class who are so inclined can pronounce their ideologies or interests.

PREJUDICE AND POLITICS

By the end of 1973 several leading American cities had elected black men as their mayors. In all those contests the voters chose the black candidate in preference to a white opponent. What happened in Cleveland, Newark, Los Angeles, Atlanta, and Detroit constitutes an important advance in American politics. First, these elections demonstrate that at least a proportion of white voters will not only cast their ballot for a black contender but will choose him over someone of their own race. Second, it shows that black citizens can and will bestir themselves to vote if they see some point in doing so. Third, it indicates that whites will still vote for the black candidate even while he serves as a symbol for black identity and aspirations. In other words, the kind of sentiments he arouses on one part of a city need not alienate voters in other parts.

New York, however, has not come near electing a black or Hispanic candidate to a city office. In fact, secondary positions have so far been beyond their reach. In 1969 Charles Rangel, the Harlem congressman, ran for the City Council president nomination in that year's Democratic primary. He finished sixth in a field of six and attracted 70,382 votes, or 10 percent of the citywide total. Even in his home borough, the headquarters of urban liberalism, he came in fifth out of six. In 1973 Joseph Galiber, a Bronx state senator, entered the Democratic primary for comptroller and did no better than Rangel. Herman Badillo's experience in 1969 and 1973 has already been mentioned.

The city has had all-white slates because so far only white entrants have come in first in the party primaries. Were candidacies determined in smoke-filled rooms, one or the other of the major parties might bestow the nomination on one of its black or Latin members. But it takes only a few petitions to get a primary scheduled, and the Democrats can always count on such a contest. At least one white liberal will always insist on running, thus siphoning off the support any black or Hispanic aspirant needs for the nomination. As long as a Mailer or Blumenthal enters, a black or Spanish-speaking frontrunner seems unlikely. The city contains a not inappreciable quotient of liberal voters who apparently prefer candidates of their own race. Their lack of enthusiasm for Rangel, Galiber, and Badillo ensured that the nominations went elsewhere.

But even a two-person contest, as with the Beame–Badillo runoff, brought a large outpouring of white voters who wished to make certain that the Democratic nominee would be one of their own race. Hence the question arises whether that part of the electorate that takes part in selecting the candidates will ever dispose itself toward a black or Hispanic politician. New York is still primarily a white city. Whites make up 73 percent of the voting-age population. They are twice as likely to vote in the average district and four times as likely in some other districts. Relative to its population, New York has fewer black and Spanish-speaking residents than any cities that have elected black mayors. Los Angeles has somewhat fewer blacks than New York (18 versus 21 percent), but its combined black and Hispanic population exceeds New York's (41 to 35 percent). Bradley did not receive many votes from Los Angeles' Latins; his victory was due chiefly to the large number of whites willing to back him. It seems inconceivable that white New Yorkers will not someday support a black candidate, especially if he runs against a white who is demonstrably less qualified for the job.

Here the legacy of 1966 shows its staying power. As has been indicated, the message enunciated through the review board referendum was that white voters would resist any attempts by blacks and Latins to assume a situation of control, whether the setting happened to be the schools, the streets, or in politics. Accordingly, any black or Spanish-speaking candidate, no matter how traditionally tailored, becomes identified with raucous and radical positions. (Were Herman Badillo to win, these imaginings ran, leather-jacketed gangs from the South Bronx would roam across the city, pushing respectable citizens off the sidewalks.) In other settings, black candidates have been able to dissociate themselves from more militant voices. Cleveland and Los Angeles and Atlanta have never known the kind of militancy common in New York. No other city, for example, has experienced pressure for school decentralization or the devolution of authority to local boards with black and Latin majorities. So long as this stridency remains part of the city scene, white voters will react as they did in the Beame–Badillo primary.

In New York it seems impossible for a black mayoral candidate to be judged on his "merits." No matter what he himself may say or do, he is cast as symbolizing a struggle over who will control the streets of the city. Perhaps so heady a mise-en-scène would have arisen even had civilian review never been put to the voters. Nevertheless, the terms of reference which began in that balloting have penetrated New York's political thinking. Any attempts toward a reformulation confront a history possessing deep roots and committed adherents.

Time can bring changes, though. The white segment of New York's population is older and growing smaller. Two-thirds of the city's Puerto Ricans and close to 60 percent of its blacks are still under 30 years of age. As they advance in years they will inevitably become a larger part of the electorate. At the same time, 60 percent of New Yorkers under 30 are neither black nor Puerto Rican; that largely white component can be counted on to vote without prodding or extra inducements.[3] Even if the city develops a black and Latin majority, the odds are still good that the white minority will prevail at the polls for quite some time. Not the least reason for this is that the nonwhite races have shown serious signs of fractionating. The 1970 Census found New York to have 1,668,115 blacks and 1,016,500 Puerto Ricans, and there is no overwhelming evidence that they will support one another's candidates. In addition the city contains 160,720 Asians; first- and second-generation arrivals from Cuba, Colombia, the Dominican Republic, and other Latin American countries contribute 233,785 local residents. These figures do not include 190,870 black New Yorkers whose parents or they themselves were born abroad. An entrant of Puerto Rican origin cannot assume that he has automatic votes on his side just because he is not white.

One consequence of a politics dominated by one race is that people will react to their lack of power in various ways. Street crime is one consequence; strikes, demonstrations, and vandalism are others. If politics in New York continue in their traditional form despite critical social and human changes, discontent will express itself in some other way.

4

A City of Communities?

The Lindsay years coincided with the spread of sociology. Vocabularies that were once confined to academe became popular. People discovered that they were "alienated," that their society was "anomic," that "crises of identity" abounded. It came as no surprise—especially under an administration as sociological as Lindsay's—to see New Yorkers drawn to the concept of *community* as a remedy for individual powerlessness and depersonalized relations.

While agreement on this value often approached unanimity, that consensus lasted only as long as the principle was not reduced to particulars. In fact, proponents of community could disagree fundamentally on how best to distribute power. They also diverged in their basic approach to citizenship. Few who called for community made explicit the rules of conduct they thought were required for such a restoration. If New York is to move effectively in this direction, more rigorous attention will have to focus on the character of people who will form the citizenry of a more communal city.

The quest for community reflects at least two disparate approaches to urban life. One looks at communities primarily in cultural terms, while the other stresses their political potential. Whereas at first glance these emphases do not appear incompatible, their premises concerning attitudes and behavior rely on different assumptions about how individuals fill the role of community citizens.

72

Until fairly recently most commentaries on community life focused on its cultural component. The city was viewed as a series of enclaves whose residents shared common values, attitudes, and perhaps heritages. "The City contains hundreds of neighborhoods, each with unique characteristics as distinctive as those of separate cities," Wallace S. Sayre and Herbert Kaufman wrote of New York in 1960. "People of the same background tend to congregate, and thus give each area, such sub-community, its special flavor."[1] Hence the emphasis on neighborhoods of common ethnic origin such as the Greek settlement in Astoria, the Norwegian colony of Sunset Park, and Italian concentrations in Belmont or Bensonhurst. Some, like Corona and Woodside, were seen almost as Old World villages where a girl married the boy down the block and grandparents owned the house just across the street. Life was friendly, trusting, and familiar. Each family understood that this was their territory.

On other occasions, associational aspects are underlined—the churches and temples, schools and social centers, which bring people together in shared activity. Often the emphasis is simply on informal contacts over beer and coffee, or backyards and front stoops, expressing the need that human beings have for one another's company. In Corona, as one resident put it, you can "walk through the streets and greet every other person as a friend or neighbor."[2] Infusing this argument is the assumption that this is what most New Yorkers want. "The people who live in them," the City Planning Commission said of many middle-class areas, "*like* their neighborhoods."[3] The appeal was that existing communities should be preserved and protected and that districts lacking such an atmosphere be assisted in creating it.

Common usage distinguishes between *neighborhoods* and *communities*. Virtually all of New York's residential blocks can be placed in one neighborhood or another, if only because most of the city's topography retains the titles of estates and villages from earlier eras. The City Planning Commission found it possible to produce a map carrying the names of no fewer than 298 neighborhoods within the boroughs' boundaries. These range from large, well-known districts such as Flushing and Flatbush in Brooklyn to locations such as Norwood and Van Nest in the Bronx, Auburndale and Briarwood in Queens, and Grymes Hill

on Staten Island. When asked *where* they live, most New Yorkers
will probably reply with a neighborhood name—although not all
can. Apart from the blocks known as Yorkville, Manhattan's
Upper East Side remains anonymous territory. In other cases
such as Brooklyn's Flatlands, residents seldom use the available
sobriquet. Because neighborhoods have no statutory boundaries,
some householders must aver that they live more or less "between" Borough Park and Bay Ridge or in the penumbra where
Williamsbridge blends into Edenwald.

Obviously neighborhoods spread themselves across a spectrum, representing a wide range of intimacy and interaction.
Some make no pretense to being communities. Residents of
Riverdale or Murray Hill may encounter smiles of recognition
when they enter certain shops or encounter their fellow tenants
in the elevator, but casual recognition does not signify community in any serious sense. Individuals living in Chelsea or Brooklyn
Heights may enjoy the sensation of seeing people with tastes or
appearances not unlike their own as they stroll on nearby streets.
This uniformity is not enough to turn a neighborhood into a
community any more than is the assertion by local residents that
they comprise a "community." As often as not, such utterances
are a strategy for rebuffing outside authority. Forest Hills, with
its high-rise apartments and the diffused involvements of its
inhabitants, can never be a community in the sense that Brooklyn's Mill Basin or Queens' College Point can. Similarly, Harlem's variations in values, classes, and cultures precludes its being
a community in any save the fact that its residents are either
black or Latin.

One way to measure the depth of community involvement
is to inquire how much of its members' lives center on their
immediate surroundings. Living side by side is not enough. *Community* calls for personal relationships of some intensity—family
attachments, associational bonds, shared values, feelings of
friendship and obligation. People enter into and become a community as they come to know one another and do things together.
By the same token, the bestowal of community membership calls
for some measure of reciprocity. Some recognizable quotient of
a person's time must be given over to his local setting even if only
in affecting an interest in the activities of one's neighbors. (How

many hours each week did Paul Goodman and Norman Mailer, two of the city's most prominent protagonists of *community*, spend commingling with their fellow residents of Cobble Hill and Chelsea?) An obvious indifference from too many household-ers is the chief impediment to community creation.

New York has enclaves where several generations of a single family live side by side and where schools, churches, and syna-gogues enlist the emotions and energies of local residents. For hundreds of thousands of wage earners, the city consists of only two centers: their place of employment and their neighborhoods. They may work in midtown Manhattan or downtown Brooklyn, but each evening they return to the Edenwalds and Edgemeres of the city. For their wives, the neighborhood may be the single focus, with few trips beyond its confines over several months. (Over 40 percent of Brooklyn's and Staten Island's residents work in their home borough.) To be a "neighborhood New Yorker," then, is to be less a denizen of the entire city than of one of its circumscribed segments.

Perhaps the chief precondition for a neighborhood's remain-ing a community is the willingness of its younger members to continue to live there even after they marry and have children of their own. Such an attachment calls for deemphasized ambi-tions, however. If individuals aspire to earnings and attainments greater than those of their friends and fathers, they may find themselves less than satisfied with surroundings they have out-grown. New York's true communities consist largely of areas where few sons or daughters rise above the lower middle class, and where most end their education at high school. The satisfac-tions found in such surroundings can compensate for rewards which remain unwon due to individuals' reluctance to test them-selves in more competitive settings. For example, families in Astoria recently opened a new Greek Orthodox high school, suggesting a preference for a more familiar schooling than the sort offered at, say, the Bronx High School of Science or Manhat-tan's Music and Art.

It is not enough to contend that the neighborhood focus makes for security, stability, and a more acquiescent and agreea-ble atmosphere. It must also be argued that this way of life has more to recommend it, for those years allotted to us, than do other alternatives. Any policy that seeks to strengthen New York's neighborhoods into coherent communities carries with it a whole series of prescriptions on how best to find personal fulfillment. Assessments of this sort become particularly evident in discussions of neighborhoods and people who prefer to limit their horizons to them. Many commentators see such citizens as a force for common sense and stability. They may not be terribly sophisticated by cosmopolitan standards, but they work hard, accept their responsibilities, and their hopes and fears deserve our attention. For example, there is Jimmy Breslin's reference to "the job-holding, churchgoing, television-watching, car-polishing, honest, bitter, loyal, unaware, clean, respectful, hung-up home-owners and small-apartment-house renters who make Queens as it was, as it is, and perhaps as it always will be."[4] But also slipping through, at least on occasion, is the additional presumption that most people should *want* to pass their years this way. The premises underlying this value are not always made clear.

If most urban dwellers were to make their neighborhoods the focus of their lives, the city as a whole would be a more orderly place. If people remained in territory of their own choosing, there would be far less of the kind of discord that arises when conflicting styles and sensibilities come in too close contact. Satisfaction with a neighborhood environment suggests that expectations will remain relatively low-keyed. This perception places a premium on a population amenable to public authority and civic order.

It is difficult not to appear patronizing. Take one case in point. During 1969 and 1970 the *New York Times* sent members of its staff to far-flung parts of the city, asking them to report on how New Yorkers live in the outlying settlements. Writing as sympathetically as they knew how, these reporters sought to tell their Manhattan-based readers what life on the urban fringe is like: ASTORIA'S UNEASY MELTING POT, NOSTALGIA ON PARK SLOPE, MASPETH FEELS FORGOTTEN, WOODSIDE'S IRISH LILT, BELMONT: A BIT OF ITALY IN THE BRONX, PELHAM PARKWAY IS AN URBAN SHTETL.[5] Despite their diligence, these Manhattan-based observers found it hard to discover much that was interesting about the neighborhoods they visited. Mike's General Store in Maspeth may have a different atmosphere from that of the Egidio Pastry

Shop in Belmont or the Penrod Stationery Store on Lydig Avenue. Young people in Beechurst played guitars and smoked grass in Clearview Park, while their counterparts in Woodside marched in the Boys' Brigade. Lower-middle-class Jews seemed to prefer the high-rise apartments of Baychester and Forest Hills, while Bensonhurst's Italians and Astoria's Greeks looked for two-family houses. Yet when it comes to explaining what people in those areas *do* with their lives, little out of the ordinary comes across. This suspicion was supported by the City Planning Commission, which concluded that a portrait gallery of a single area —Mosholu Parkway in the Bronx—sufficed to convey the character of the hundred or more middle-income sections of the city.[6] To paraphrase a novelist puzzled by a similar problem, *neighborhood people seem all alike.*

Inherent in the conception of community is the belief that if compelled to compete, most people will end up losers, not simply in economic terms but with real damage to their self-respect as well. This assumption also implies that the average citizen cannot be expected to create his own associative life. Better that he be presented with a neighborhood community where the fabric has already been woven and is ready to receive him. To imply that "most people" will be happiest in an encapsulated neighborhood shielded from the competition and variety of a fast-moving world assumes that it is safest not to expose individuals to hazards with which they cannot cope. Yet no one can know how many would succeed or fail were they put to the test. Many neighborhood New Yorkers have never really tried.

It can also be argued that such depictions are essentially conservative insofar as their stress is on a congenial culture rather than the exercise of power. The accent on common habits and sidewalk sociability deflects attention from the fact that local residents rarely participate in decisions on major matters. Since the conventional community portrayal allows for politics, electing representatives on the basis of ethnic origins means that substantive issues remain outside the purview of politics. As often as not, officeholders chosen for their ethnicity support the prevailing structure, notably values agreeable to the business community. If such constituencies enjoy an agreeable atmosphere, it is because issues which might prove divisive seldom emerge. Blame for anxiety and insecurity is usually directed at "outsiders" rather than the lack of rewards and opportunities within a small neighborhood.

An air of nostalgia tends to pervade this picture. Residents appear contented with their place and refrain from demands that might imperil the underlying structure. If community citizens cause little trouble it is because they settle for exercising only a modest influence within a delimited definition of politics. In short, these people cause little trouble. "The major reason Queens residents were so passive so long," Murray Schumach has pointed out, "was that they thought of themselves as belonging primarily to their community."[7]

An opposing view posits that life in a circumscribed setting hinders personal development: a person born in this half of the century should not be content to subsist simply as a citizen of Seagate or St. Albans when he has the opportunity to live in a wider, more diversified world. This thesis evidently is what Catherine Bauer had in mind when she wrote that a neighborhood emphasis can be "reactionary in effect and sentimental in concept."[8] Her assumption is that individuals possess the potential to become part of a greater society, that their capacity for realization should be liberated from local customs and constrictions. In this evaluation the urban neighborhood emerges as the contemporary equivalent of the rural village, founded on ritual rather than reflection and expressing social immobility instead of opportunity and introspection. Donald Cook is another who has expressed this view:

> The "neighborhood" . . . is usually presented as a relatively stable semi-ethnic slum that gives a good deal of satisfaction to those who remain in it. I would say that what is most characteristically urbane about the city is not the neighborhood.
>
> One of the transformations we shall continue to witness is precisely the destruction of this comfortable, self-contained social entity. Indeed, I think that its loss may be a good thing, from the point of view of the more exciting prospects of city life.[9]

This view is shared by hundreds of thousands of younger New Yorkers brought up in neighborhoods but who elect not to raise their own families in such settings. Some decline to return because their adolescent surroundings have become lower-class slums. Others retreat to the suburbs, abandoning urban life altogether. For example, while Queens' high schools send quite a few of their graduates to Ivy League colleges, hardly any return. (Taken together, the neighborhoods of Astoria, Cambria Heights, Howard Beach, Laurelton, Maspeth, Rego Park, Rockaway Beach, and Woodhaven house a total of *nine* Princeton graduates.)[10] There is reason to believe that the coming generation of New Yorkers has more expansive ideas about the kind of people they want to be, with their friends and associations chosen not by neighborhood proximity but for shared concerns that transcend being brought up on the same block or having grandparents from similar backgrounds.

The vision of community described thus far is essentially nonpolitical. Not its least attraction lies in the premise that, given a comfortable culture, citizens feel no compulsion to argue issues of governance. But passivity of this sort can no longer be assumed. The average New Yorker now expects more attention and more extensive benefits than his counterpart of the past. As never before, he feels free to criticize the administration and allocation of both public and private services. Such a tendency cannot help but lead to questions about how power is being exercised within the city. Given this new sensitivity, New Yorkers react by demanding a greater share in the arena of influence. Local residents demand immunity from outside impositions and the right to administer institutions lying within their localities. New York's neighborhoods have ceased being placid villages. Once guarantors of a restrained citizenry, they now appear as contentious cockpits.

A few examples are in order. Given a land area of approximately 300 square miles, most of the city's residents will grant that space can be found for new public amenities—on the condition that they be located far away from their own neighborhoods. One of the surest ways to mobilize "community feeling" is for a public agency or private institution to propose building an installation in a particular area. Even if such an intrusion does not require razing homes or businesses, the odds are still high that local householders will protest. Within a single five-month period as the city moved into the 1970s, cries of outrage were heard from

Pelham Parkway in the Bronx to Paerdegat Basin in Brooklyn.

In early February 1970 an overflow crowd of several hundred Inwood residents met to register their rage over a "marine gar-bage-transfer facility" planned for 215th Street at the Harlem River. Between 300 and 600 Department of Sanitation trucks would come through each day to dump their loads onto barges. "I'm prepared to go to jail over this, and there are people who will follow me," said an officer of the Inwood Civic Council. "Now we're a community. We're as one."[11]

In mid-March 1970 300 residents of Bayside marched out-side Fort Totten to protest the use of that century-old army base as a Job Corps training center for 250 youths, chiefly from ghetto areas. One of the organizers threatened to enlist "a brigade of middle-class mothers to lie down in front of the bulldozers."[12] Actually, bulldozers were not necessary; only internal renovations of the building were needed.

The previous November students and householders from Morningside Heights disrupted an Atomic Energy Commission hearing convened to consider Columbia University's request to operate a nuclear reactor on its campus. "We have been too mistreated to believe what Columbia University says," a member of the Morningside Tenants Committee said after hearing assur-ances of absolute safety. "I've never seen the community so unanimous as it is on this point," added a local politician.[13]

By the end of January 1970 the Lindenwood Civic Associa-tion had secured 3,500 signatures for a petition opposing con-struction of a low-income housing project in the Howard Beach section of Queens. A local rabbi pointed out that the new resi-dents would not "blend in" with the neighborhood's $50,000 homes. He was asked at a Board of Estimate hearing, "where are they to go—these people who want to get out of the ghettoes—if every time plans are made to help them, a community says it does not want them?" The leader of the congregation replied, "I am sorry that there are ghettoes, but that is the way it is."[14]

In November 1969 the Bronx Community Council of Pel-ham Parkway North helped to fill the Christopher Columbus auditorium for a meeting that went on past midnight. The reason was a 200-by-230-foot lot on which the Board of Education planned to build an occupational training center for 400 mentally retarded young adults. Among the objections: "It's not fair to subject the trainees to some of the abuse and teasing our children can give them." Perhaps this was not the best of all possible places for such a center, an official admitted, adding: "but to wait for the ideal site is like waiting for the ideal society."[15]

The Wavecrest Civic Association, the Seagirt Civic Improvement Association, the Wavecrest Gardens Community Association, the Senior Citizens Civic Association, the Far Rockaway Taxpayers and Civic Association, and the Lawrence Green Civic Association all called on Mayor Lindsay to close Far Rockaway's Phoenix House rehabilitation center for former drug addicts in December. Petitions, claimed to be signed by 75 percent of the registered voters in the area, charged that continuation of the center would be "the first nail in the coffin towards a deterioration of our community."[16]

In December 1970 there was a midtown Manhattan picket line demonstrating against construction of an Alexander's branch store at Broadway and 96th Street. "If we let Alexander's build, other stores will follow suit and our neighborhood as we know it will be completely destroyed," said a state senator who joined the protest. "This is the beginning of a grab by the real estate guys and banks," claimed a local priest. "What we want is a small renaissance, a neighborhood with small stores and boutiques," a district leader added. But Alexander's doubted that the opposition ran deep. "In the West Side, there are self-styled leaders with phantom constituencies," according to one of their vice-presidents.[17]

At the other end of the city, the Joint Council for Local Betterment—speaking for civic groups in Bergen Beach, Flatlands, Mill Basin, and Paerdegat Basin—brought out a crowd of rain-soaked citizens on a December Sunday in 1970 to protest a proposed shopping center at Flatbush Avenue and the Belt Parkway, which would bring 50,000 vehicles a day into the area. A local medical expert warned the City Planning Commission that the ensuing air pollution, in topography of this kind, could cause a "health emergency."[18]

Activity of this sort is evidence of the increasing tendency of New Yorkers of all races and classes to mobilize themselves to

affect the exercise of power in New York City. Alongside preex-
isting civic, social, and charitable endeavors, there has grown up
a network of local organizations that are frankly political in purpose. While these associations address themselves to elected
officeholders and attempt to enlist their support, their methods
and motivations are far more freewheeling than those of conventional politics.

It is impossible to say just when this development started,
but one landmark was the day about a decade ago when upper-
middle-class mothers on the West Side embarked on direct action, mobilizing their baby carriages to prevent the displacement
of a Central Park playground by a parking lot intended for the
Tavern-on-the-Green. In other parts of the city, activist associations have taken more concrete form. In addition to countless
health, tenants, and parents groups can be added quasi-official
watchdog bodies such as the Park Slope Civic Council, the East-
chester Community Homeowners Association, and the Veronica
Place Block Association—all prepared to investigate, litigate, and
demand a more effective response by authorities. Many New
Yorkers are prepared to occupy schools, hospitals, and welfare
offices to dramatize their desire for better services. Generally
speaking, the procedure is to mount as vocal a protest as possible
against the proposals, decisions, or inattention of distantly admin-
istered agencies. If sufficient numbers are mustered and enough
noise is made, if local spirits can be kept ignited and countervail-
ing forces are indecisive, the city's bureaucracies may possibly be
responsive. Quite clearly, this kind of activity carries serious constitutional implications, going far beyond the normal practices of
pressure and petitioning.

In earlier days New Yorkers were likely to accept the level
of services the city provided, not because the quality was better
but because citizens' conception of what they were entitled to
was less expansive. (In the 1930s, for example, rush-hour crowding in the subways was even worse than it is now.) Householders
never thought it was their place to convene committees to complain over these and other inconveniences. Nor will it do to claim
that precinct captains mediated citizen grievances to any appre-
ciable degree. Interventions of this sort doubtless occurred, but
they were not nearly so frequent as many would like to believe,

and they were seldom directed at the overall pattern of public service. A party official might arrange a release from jail, but he did not temper the backroom brutality so common in the city's police stations.

During the Lindsay years there arose the notion of a new-style politics which would decentralize decision-making and, more importantly, seek to involve as many New Yorkers as possible in this process. The terms *neighborhood* and *community* came to connote a participating citizenry whose consent must be enlisted before anyone could implement policies that will affect their lives. The devolution of power is obviously an attractive idea. As early as 1969, 62 percent of the respondents questioned in a *Daily News* poll supported "more control for local neighborhoods," while only 17 percent wanted less, with the remainder wanting to keep things as they were.[19] John Lindsay seemed to share this sentiment. "We cannot plan for the citizenry unless we plan with them," he wrote after the 1969 election, "unless we are willing to give to individuals, to neighborhoods, and to communities the power to be heard and the power to challenge, the power most of all to decide as much as possible what their communities will look like and how they will work."[20] This message was carried across the city by members of his administration. On one such mission late in 1969, a staff member of the City Planning Commission went to Sheepshead Bay to tell a hundred assembled householders that "while communities may not get everything they want, there will be a mutual veto so that the city cannot impose its wishes without their approval."[21]

Perhaps officials should have thought twice before uttering such promises. Did they really mean that *every community* would be allowed to veto facilities proposed for their neighborhood? As indicated above, when administrators selected Inwood as the site of a new garbage-collection depot, the local uproar could be heard across three rivers. On this issue, at least, the neighborhood united in its opposition, leading a beleaguered representative from City Hall to reply: "they have to remember that Inwood is not a village. It is part of the city. Each neighborhood has to have its share of the undesirable work of the city, or else we're not a city, just a collection of villages."[22] The charm of community creation began to wear off as sections like Inwood began to

acquire a measure of power. But rather than repudiate the entire
principle of community—local attachments might once again
serve to promote passivity—questioning the credentials of com-
plainants became a more prudent tactic. "The city has made very
clear that until it is satisfied that a particular community group
is representative and makes known what it wants, the city isn't
going to do anything," an official asserted.[23] In effect, one could
favor community autonomy in principle but still question its
legitimacy in application. It is evident that the city has no shortage of individuals prepared to style themselves spokesmen for the
"community." How is anyone to know whether a committee, a
picket line, or a demonstration reflects general sentiment in an
area? So far as is possible, the system tries to channel expressions
of opinion into the electoral process. Let those with a grievance
put their own people into public office. Only by winning an
election may a person claim representative status. The political
structure not only provides legitimacy, it also seeks to maintain
a monopoly of authority. Hence the advice to complaining citizens that they come up with candidates pledged to new policies.
Rather than facing pressure from the streets, it is better to absorb
that energy in council chambers.

During the Lindsay administration the city saw the creation
of a whole series of elective agencies: 32 school boards, 26 pover-
ty-area corporations, and 12 or more model cities and hospital
boards. Not surprisingly, the turnouts for these elections have
been very low, with a 15-percent-participation rate being the
upper limit in most neighborhoods. Yet from one vantage point,
15 percent is not an unimpressive figure, considering the patch-
work of overlapping jurisdictions, the irregularity of elections,
and the information and interest necessary to evaluate candidates
for various positions. At the same time, these low turnouts have
strengthened the claim that even elected bodies do not speak the
sentiments of local residents. School boards embracing predominantly black areas have ended up with white majorities. Poverty
corporation boards in all-black neighborhoods were frequently
dominated by persons with special affiliations or interests. "They
were not generalized spokesmen for the poor," one commentator
claimed of those elected to the corporation boards. "They tended
to be the newer, younger, more militant, more chauvinistic wing

of the old civil rights movement."[24] But criticism of this sort carries no more authority than the assertions of self-appointed spokesmen. An outside observer who claims that an elected board is not representative must produce some evidence that he has conducted a better head count. When all is said and done, there is no foolproof way of discovering the sentiments of people who fail to vote.

Still, the notion persists that New Yorkers can be transformed into constituencies of responsible citizens. According to this conviction, they can be induced to give greater amounts of their time and energy to attending meetings, discussing issues, and informing themselves on the growing array of candidates for the boards, councils, and committees that touch their neighborhoods. Such committed citizens would vote for, keep tabs on, and reward or punish the members of at least a dozen community and legislative bodies, at the same time fragmenting their political identities to fit the contours of several unsynchronized constituencies.[25] Yet, given the feelings of impatience, frustration, and injustice so pervasive in this period of the city's history, it seems academic to expect that New Yorkers will settle into so subdued a concept of citizenship. For this reason, no attempt will be made here to comment on various proposals for decentralizing administrative services or assigning these functions to neighborhood councils. Suffice it to say that hardly a week passes without the appearance of some new report recommending yet another devolutionary plan.[26]

By the same token, opposition to decentralization and community control stems from diverse sources. On one hand are officials of citywide unions, fearful that teachers, firemen, or hospital employees may become vulnerable to locally elected employers. This was the lesson of the Ocean Hill–Brownsville imbroglio of 1968; it caused the Patrolmen's Benevolent Association to join forces not only with the United Federation of Teachers but also the Real Estate Board of New York in seeking to preserve the uniformities to which they had become accustomed. Allied with them is an older style of liberal: those committed to precepts of rational administration and who think dispersion is inefficient and amateurism a danger. Consultants, systems analysts, and advocates of professionalized management worry lest their achievements be jeopardized by local residents unable to appreciate sophisticated approaches.

Yet the fact remains that more people than in the past feel entitled to share in the exercise of power. What will be considered here are some of the attempts to awaken community consciousness and assess the reactions to these efforts once the movement was underway. During the greater part of John Lindsay's tenure, the focus was on remedying the fact and feeling of powerlessness within New York's low-income neighborhoods.

At the beginning of the 1960s a growing number of observers were becoming disturbed over the fact that participation was so exclusively a middle-class preserve. The question began to be asked why a wider section of the citizenry, especially the poor, did not take part in the arena of influence. Perhaps the most popular analysis was that suggested by Oscar Lewis: the "culture of poverty" so depressed its members as to disbar them from the political life. "It is, on the whole, a comparatively superficial culture," Lewis said. "Its pervading mistrust magnifies individual helplessness and isolation. Indeed, poverty of culture is one of the crucial traits of the culture of poverty."[27] Peter Marris expanded on this thesis, underscoring the alienating effect of being poor:

> The poor man not only fails to comprehend society or his community: he is out of touch with it. He reads fewer newspapers, hears fewer programs, joins fewer organizations, and knows less of the current life of either the community or the larger world than more prosperous better educated people do. Nor do the poor associate among themselves more than minimally. Experiencing separation from society and each other, it is natural for them to feel alone and detached. And feeling no identity even with each other, they view the world as indifferent and distant.[28]

And Lola Irelan stressed the disorganization she saw as characteristic of the slum setting:

> It has no leaders, few community associations, no means of asserting a common purpose. It may not even be very neighborly, as neighborliness is understood in the suburbs. It is held together as a community only by its hostility to the world outside, and lacks any integrating organization.[29]

Generalizations of this sort no longer go unanswered. Many authorities are now prepared to respond that lower-class neighborhoods have a vibrancy missing in more sedate areas, that despite the violence and drug addiction in the slums, there is a display of cooperation and consanguinity seldom found in other parts of the city. Alongside the dangers of darkened hallways stands a full panoply of associational activity, ranging from churches and scout troops to gambling clubs and the friendly socializing on front stoops. In consequence, it could be asserted that the human potential was available and only needed to be brought to the surface through a new series of structures. For the poor to join the participatory process, it was proposed, the pump must first be primed with public funds. What was especially needed was an echelon of individuals to organize the residents of local areas. As poor people lacked personnel with the resources to challenge prevailing centers of power, the solution was to create neighborhood leaders by paying them salaries and supplying funds for offices and the other appurtenances of associational endeavor.

John Lindsay offered one of the country's warmest welcomes to the newly created Community Action Programs. Although mayors in many other cities saw these agencies as threats to their organizations, Lindsay did not have a political structure that needed protection from competition. Through the Office of Economic Opportunity there came into being the neighborhood "corporation." These differed from conventional associations in that, while they did not have to rely on levying dues, they could still deploy officials to mobilize sentiment on issues of local interest. By the beginning of 1970 more than 14,000 people were receiving salaries from 26 neighborhood organizations, ranging from the Lower East Side Community Corporation, the Downtown Brooklyn Development Corporation, and the Crown Heights Community Corporation (the latter having a $700,000 appropriation and 30 employees) to the Chelsea Action Center, Harlem Teams for Self-Help, and the Hunts Point Multi-Service Center (the last with a $4,000,000 budget, an $18,000-a-year director, and a payroll approaching 300). One result of such subsidies was the creation of a new occupational category, the "povertycrat" who more or less combined the functions of trade union organizer, association lobbyist, and party worker with a patronage job.

What, in fact, did these corporations *do?* Although part of the "War on Poverty" program, they did not actually give government money to the poor—apart from the individuals serving on their salaried staffs. Rather, corporation funds were spent on organizing—bringing people together in new activities, helping them to redefine their own interests and aspirations, creating a consciousness of their place and prerogatives in the larger society. More money was spent on renting premises, running duplicating machines, and paying for postage and telephones. The purpose of these expenditures was to accelerate the process whereby poor New Yorkers arrived at a new conception of themselves and their rights as citizens.

There appeared cadet corps for teenagers, discussion groups for older people, theatre groups, and even trips to New England ski resorts for young children. (The latter outlay was rationalized on the ground that if offspring of the well-to-do can have such experiences, why not youngsters from the slums?) In association with Headstart groups, day-care centers, and school associations, the corporations sought to work with parents, awakening them to demands they had not hitherto known could be made on the educational system. In alliance with federally funded law offices, they encouraged litigation against landlords, merchants, and public agencies whose procedures ran counter to prevailing statutes.

If the intention of these "action" programs was to raise consciousness and create communities, it is difficult to measure their overall effectiveness. Figures on how many people were "reached" by such activities are not significant. An individual who received a prescription at a storefront clinic or another who joined a discussion on garbage collection was counted in such statistics. At the same time, the corporation could be credited with informing people of their rights under existing legislation. Faced with charges that his administration was responsible for expanding the city's welfare rolls, Lindsay remarked: "it is not right to say that the city encouraged people to go on welfare. Community action groups did that. They dug out the most severe poverty of all the persons who were festering in sickness, and brought the whole mess up to the surface."[30]

Whether the Brownsville Community Council or the East Harlem Triangle were able to solidify the scattered residents of

Brownsville and East Harlem into a "community" remains unanswered. A certain fraction of local New Yorkers—more than ever
in the past—became involved in the exercise of power. But it is
not easy to speak of community corporation officials as "leaders"
in the usual sense. They operate as much from platforms they
themselves have created (with the help of federal money) as they
do for the constituencies their corporations embrace.

It may well be that the appearance of so many cross-cutting
and overlapping corporations, block associations, tenant associations, parents associations, and health associations, militates
against community solidarity at the local level. For example,
there have been endless arguments in the Chelsea-Village Health
Council constituency over who should exert influence in the
administration of St. Vincent's Hospital. In Crown Heights,
Hasidic Jews battled blacks over the priorities involved in federally funded poverty programs, and in the South Bronx, blacks
contended with Puerto Ricans for control of multimillion dollar
budgets. One city official estimated that in a 12-month period,
over $150 million in funds available for public construction went
unspent due to conflicts over who was to sit in positions of
power.[31]

In several of the city's low-income areas battle lines have
emerged around the schools, where local boards have the authority to hire and fire substantial numbers of employees, ranging
from principals and program directors to teacher's aides and
cafeteria workers. With the closing out of federal money for
poverty programs, the patronage potential in a decentralized
school system took up much of the slack in neighborhoods where
white-collar jobs are scarce. Here, too, frequent charges arise that
the boards fail to represent the entire area and instead have
become the preserve of individuals who make a successful sweep
in ill-attended elections.

Acts of assertion such as these have aroused concern among
observers committed to more orthodox political procedures. Put
most simply, the indictment is that the city has become too
democratic, with too many participants and too much participation. Roger Starr has referred scathingly to "the belief that the
consent of the governed . . . must be sought, not in general and
at election times, but in the case of every issue affecting the lives

of the citizens significantly."[32] In a parallel analysis Herbert Kaufman saw in this impulse not simply a demand for more responsiveness from public officials or even the power to apply pressure on them, but a wholesale restructuring of administrative arrangements:

> Neighborhood groups . . . seek more than influence on the behavior of public officials and employees; they call for delegation to *themselves* of public power over programs, finances, and administrative structure. They no longer want just to tell the city government what to do; they want to *be* the government that does it.[33]

To this tocsin, Midge Decter added the opinion that "the fashionable new cry for community control . . . is in fact the expression of the wish—a reactionary wish—to have one's local demands taken out of that large central sphere where men of political bent are forced to reconcile them with the demands of others."[34]

Critiques such as these are usually accompanied by the assumption that participation should confine itself to the ballot box, democracy's mechanism for replacing unsatisfactory incumbents with people more attuned to constituency sentiment. More particularly, citizens are reminded of their opportunity to work through the political parties. Clubhouses, reform groups, and primary candidates welcome the arrival of any citizen willing to donate his time and effort, and such service eventually provides access to circles where decisions are made.[35] It is for this reason that Nathan Glazer and Daniel Patrick Moynihan wrote reprovingly of "the failure of Negroes and Puerto Ricans to develop and seize the political opportunities that were open to them."[36]

The reason so many New Yorkers find working through party channels unappealing is that the parties are not set up to deal with the kind of problems neighborhoods now face. Even if citizens organized to support new slates of candidates in local primaries, commandeering control in their assembly district would not restore Brownsville's tenements to good repair or rid the South Bronx of its addicts. The suspicion arises that those admonishing citizens to confine their politics to time-honored procedures feel that individuals should be satisfied with the range of reform that existing agencies are able to manage.

What is being debated is how government may best be organized in New York City. On one side are those who believe that public sentiment should be registered at the ballot box at appropriate intervals, while in the interim both officials and administrators should be permitted to carry on unimpeded with the business of governing the city. This view tends to respect the competence and credentials of professionals such as school principals, welfare administrators, and others experienced in public service.[37] The contrasting attitude celebrates popular participation in a variety of forms, ranging from petitions and picketing to more active demonstrations which can extend to occupying offices and obstructing operations. Calls for community control of public agencies carry the conviction that firsthand knowledge of a neighborhood's needs should take priority over formal training and citywide personnel policies.

The traditional picture of neighborhood New York as a series of acquiescent enclaves has been drastically altered. This phenomenon has been called "para-politics," a more vigorous form of petitioning wherein property and procedures are accorded less respect than was once the case. Neither public nor private institutions have the strength to ignore such demands or to punish those dramatizing them. New York's centers of authority were never intended to deal with para-political expression of such intensity and magnitude.

It is all too easy to assign the blame to politicians or union officials, to welfare recipients or construction workers, to local leaders or would-be leaders. It is even easier to identify as the chief culprits sedentary intellectuals supposedly entranced by flying bottles and burning garbage.[38] The incapacity of the city's government to satisfy its constituents is an inescapable fact, yet it is by no means clear that New York can be turned into a series of smaller communities in which citizens control their public fortunes. The very traits that have brought para-political rebellions against established institutions will also surface in the councils and committees at local levels.

If the experiment is to be attempted, it is important to draw attention to a phenomenon that will come into greater prominence if neighborhoods are accorded greater powers of self-government. This is the tendency, already common in small

towns and suburbs, for more fortunate areas to renounce responsibility for problems outside their jurisdiction. Large segments of
the population—the aged and infirm, as well as the addicted,
delinquent, and dependent—are not evenly distributed throughout the whole society. Instead, they are concentrated in certain
parts of the country, achieving their highest visibility in the slums
of the nation's largest cities. The fact that most suburbs do *not*
have such people in more than token numbers becomes an obvious but unacknowledged bonus. Suburbs do not have to appropriate funds to prevent lead-paint poisoning nor do they feel any
obligation to alleviate venereal disease among innercity adolescents. The United States has permitted historical accidents to
become institutionalized, with the result that civic responsibilities end at a town or county line. If self-government means that
a locality can run its own schools and fire stations, it also means
that such a jurisdiction can veto the placement of public housing
within its boundaries.

If areas such as Williamsburg and Fort Greene became
independent, it would be important to know where they would
raise funds to deal with the problems concentrated within them.
At this point, better-off sections of the city subsidize less fortunate areas, providing welfare payments, added school services,
and special police for public housing projects. It is incumbent on
those advocating decentralization to show how such intracity
subventions would be continued. Why should College Point give
gifts to Crown Heights, any more than Bronxville gives to the
South Bronx, if College Point has no feelings of fraternity toward
Crown Heights?

Another difficulty facing those who seek to create communities lies in the fact that moves in this direction cannot be shielded from outside eyes. A critical component of the community-
building process is the willingness of its members to acknowledge
that they must solve certain problems largely by their own de-
vices. Such self-criticisms are made much easier if local debates
and discussions are shielded from onlookers in the larger society.
But in today's New York every such effort seems under continual
scrutiny, whether by legislators, researchers, or the mass media.
A neighborhood meeting need only produce one or another
speaker holding forth on the facts about local conditions, and

Channel 5, WOR, the *Daily News,* or an NYU graduate student is bound to be present. Given current preoccupations with the "image" entertained by others, there is a tendency to remain silent on subjects about which one does not wish to remind outsiders.

Take the problem of heroin addiction in black neighborhoods. Black New Yorkers, much more than whites, face burglary, robbery, and the everyday dismay that comes from the presence of addicts on stoops and street corners. To be sure, individual residents of black neighborhoods complain about this condition and its consequences for their everyday lives, but it is notable how little has been accomplished in the way of concerted action. Instead, blame is assigned elsewhere: inadequate police protection, discrimination in employment, the syndicates responsible for bringing drugs into black areas. It cannot be denied that the widespread use of heroin by blacks is ultimately a result of the way such individuals have been treated by a society consisting chiefly of a race other than their own. But what neighborhood spokesmen cannot go on to say is: "this is *our* problem, and we are going to have to deal with our own people." Much could be done by blacks, within black neighborhoods, to ameliorate addiction and to control its criminal consequences. Effective steps could be taken without outside resources. But such problems would involve mobilizing residents much more effectively than those that are presently available to work intensively with—and on—one another. Much as they were in small towns, deviants have been brought into line by local opinion and unsubtle sanctions.

In a city like New York, if a black leader seeks to invoke action by saying, "this is *our* problem," his words are immediately picked up by the white press and broadcast to white audiences. An invitation addressed to a local assemblage immediately becomes transformed into a black man's admission, heard by white ears, that many blacks are addicts. Blacks themselves know that more of their race are on heroin than is the case with other groups. But they also dislike having this fact disseminated, for it encourages stereotypes for whites to apply to the entire black population. As a result, efforts at internal mobilization, including the meetings and self-analysis which must precede such a step, have been slow to start and sporadic in success. It should be plain that white society is not going to change its treatment of black citizens in any substantial way, nor are the white media going to ignore self-criticism when it comes from black quarters. It is understandable that blacks feel obliged to concern themselves with the image their race presents to white eyes, for, after all, it is white society that provides employment and finances public services. The dilemma is a real one, and it cannot be resolved without some pain. At the same time, too defensive a posture is bound to be self-defeating.

Living in a fishbowl is hardly the best setting for community creation, especially when the areas in question have problems like premarital pregnancy, prostitution, venereal disease, and father-less households crying out for correction. But the failure of blacks themselves to articulate these matters, apart from mounting attacks on white insensitivity, means even further postponement of the time when their neighborhoods will become the kind of communities their current residents aspire to live in.

From Thomas Jefferson through the establishment of the Community Action Programs, a basic theme of the communitarian impulse has been the process of self-improvement. There is a need for better schools, more effective police, and an infusion of outside money. Yet, granting all this, self-improvement also calls for local exercises in self-analysis, which, in turn, requires that the participants ignore the presence of television cameras and take the risk that admissions made in private will become public knowledge. Unless such self-confidence is mustered, the creation or continuation of community life will remain a thwarted aspiration. Attributing neighborhood problems to outside agencies is too easy a rationalization. Even more generous provision of appropriations and attention will not correct the most chronic dangers and discomforts now in evidence. The underlying remedy lies with local activity by local residents, directed at individuals in their own backyards.

5

Classes and Conflict

The Lindsay years saw a sharp rise in ethnic, cultural, and ideological awareness, with more citizens becoming conscious of their location in the city's framework. Candidates increasingly address their constituencies by posing issues in terms of *us* versus *them*, leaving the voters to work out the connotations for themselves. When observers noted the "divisiveness" infecting New York during the Lindsay administration, they were simply saying that many of the city's conflicts had a class basis—not in the orthodox Marxian meaning, for issues of race, crime, and living styles overlay economic interests and political identification. Even so, the city could not satisfy everyone's aspirations for better incomes, personal safety, and social esteem. Each gain for one group resulted in a real or relative loss for another. Most important, these gains and losses tend to be viewed as victories or defeats for particular classes rather than as resulting from policies based on objective need or at least on accident or chance.

To the eyes of many onlookers, John Lindsay's administration seemed to delight in exacerbating grievances which had hitherto lain dormant. Before 1966 not all New Yorkers were content with their place in the city's structure, but they were not inclined to define their grievances in terms of class. In fact, on several occasions they attributed their frustrated ambitions to personal shortcomings. Neither a criminal nor a welfare class occupied prominent positions in the city; a cosmopolitan constituency had only begun to emerge. New Yorkers of all classes

95

had much in common when it came to their outlook on citizenship. Except for what was then known as the "Negro population," most people did not regard themselves as oppressed or
threatened by other sectors of the city; considering their plight
even residents of Harlem and Bedford–Stuyvesant managed to
keep their resentment muted. Before 1966 few New Yorkers felt
it their place to demand that more be bestowed on them than
was then the case. Hardly ever did anyone—certainly after the
days of Vito Marcantonio—call for a redistribution of the city's
services and resources.

The purpose of this chapter is to survey New York's classes
at the end of John Lindsay's mayoralty, focusing on various issues
in the city. From time to time some speculation will be offered
as to what would have to happen for these demands to be satisfied
—in particular, who and what would have to make room or give
way were currently aggrieved groups to attain the equities they
now desire.

WHO—AND HOW MANY—ARE POOR?

The 1970 Census, using a formula agreed on by federal
agencies, listed 1,150,685 New Yorkers as living below the poverty line. This figure represents approximately one out of every
seven of the city's residents. The federal standard requires a
severe state of deprivation for a person to be classed as poor. For
inclusion in the poverty population at the time of the 1970
Census, a city-dweller living alone had to have an annual income
of less than $1,840; a family of two could have no more than
$2,383; and the ceiling for a family of four was $3,743.[1]

Unfortunately these were the only cutoff points the Census
used for correlating personal characteristics with level of income.
The federal figures need not be accepted; they are, however, the
only statistical breakdowns available in printed form.

The analysis in Chapter 2 located 680,926 of New York's
families and 564,710 of its single individuals in the "low-income"
category, although there the dividing lines were drawn at $7,000
for a family and $5,000 for individuals. It is necessary to distin-
guish between the approximately 2,850,000 individuals who were
considered low income in Chapter 2, and who comprised 41

percent of the city and the 1,150,685 persons the Census identified as poor, who make up the bottom 40 percent of the low-
income stratum. On the whole it seems accurate to say that the
top part of the low-income group consists mainly of low-paid
wage earners, while the bottom part is composed chiefly of persons who are not gainfully employed.

Of all the people in the city, the poor are most likely to have
been overlooked by the Census. The figure of 1,150,685 understates the number of poor residents more seriously than do comparable figures for other classes. There is no way of knowing how
much larger the poverty population might be. (For example,

Table 5.1. Distribution of Poor, by Age, Race, and Family Status

	Black and Puerto Rican		White and Other Races	
Adults, 18 to 64				
male family heads	51,221	4.4%	39,359	3.4%
female family heads	82,764	7.2	21,293	1.9
other family members	83,445	7.3	66,907	5.8
persons living alone	50,724	4.4	84,915	7.4
		23.3%		18.5%
Children Under 18				
in families with male head	126,310	11.0%	61,998	5.3%
in families with female head	229,044	19.9	46,581	4.1
		30.9%		9.4%
Adults, 65 and Over	34,728	3.0	171,396	14.9
	658,236	57.2%	492,449	42.8%
Total		100%		

Urban Poverty Incomes
person living alone   under $1,840
two-person family   under 2,383
three-person family   under 2,924
four-person family   under 3,743

274,536 households located by the Census admitted receiving welfare funds, whereas the Department of Social Services had records of more than 475,000 cases in that year.) The problem, of course, is that if 1,150,685 seems too low, any alternative total would be equally open to suspicion. Once again, the official figures have the virtue of precision and the drawback of incompleteness.

Table 5.1 shows that about 40 percent of the poor are children and 18 percent are old people, leaving 42 percent who are, at least in theory, of employable age. In fact, almost half of the poor population consists either of families having a man as its head or persons between 18 and 64 who do not head a family. (Many of these "other family members" are the wives of household heads.) Families headed by women account for only one-third of the city's poor residents. More than half of New York's poor are black or Puerto Rican, with the largest of the city's categories—almost 20 percent—being children living in households headed by a woman. The second largest segment of the poverty population—about 15 percent—consists of aged white people. The third—11 percent—includes black or Puerto Rican children in families having a man present. None of the 11 remaining categories take in more than 8 percent of the city's poor.

Table 5.2 gives the proportions that poor people represent within the various groups for the city as a whole. Fully 62 percent of fatherless black and Puerto Rican children are poor, compared with only 6 percent of the city's white children who live with their fathers. Approximately 22 percent of New York's aged citizens live below the poverty line, although this figure includes only individuals receiving less than $35 a week and couples living on less than $46. (In this case, the Census regards weekly incomes of $36 and $47 as a step above poverty and does not give an analysis by age for those in higher brackets.) Using the same cutoff points, only 21 percent of the city's children belong to poor households. The figures in Table 5.2 also suggest the extent to which poverty is based on race. With age, sex, and family composition constant, higher proportions of blacks and Puerto Ricans are poor in every category. But the gaps are by no means uniform. The proportions with poverty incomes show smaller racial dis-

Table 5.2. Percentage of Poor in Various Age, Race, and Family Groups

	Black and Puerto Rican		White and Other Races	
Adults, 18 to 64				
male family heads	51,221	13%	39,359	4%
female family heads	82,764	47	21,293	17
other family members	83,445	14	66,907	4
persons living alone	50,724	27	84,915	18
Children Under 18				
in families with male head	126,310	21%	61,998	6%
in families with female head	229,044	62	46,581	37
Adults, 65 and Over	34,728	31%	171,396	21%
Total	658,236	27%	492,449	9%

Urban Poverty Incomes	
person living alone	under $1,840
two-person family	under 2,383
three-person family	under 2,924
four-person family	under 3,743

crepancies among the aged, single individuals, and children living in households headed by a woman. The racial ratios are much further apart with family heads and children in male-headed households. The availability of Social Security and welfare payments tends to diminish the income gap between the races, whereas the pay scales of employers help to keep blacks and Puerto Ricans at poverty levels. Public programs relegate racial variations to the background; in the push and pull of the job market, race differences appear to be more pronounced.

THE UNDERPAID POOR

New York, in company with other large cities, houses a disproportionate share of the nation's poor. In dollar-for-dollar terms, America's rural counties have higher ratios of their people below the poverty line. More malnutrition infects Clarendon

County, South Carolina than the South Bronx; life is considerably bleaker for most residents of Elk County, Kansas than for those living in Brooklyn's Brownsville. But contrasts of this sort, while accurate enough, provide little perspective on urban poverty. To have a low income in New York means seeing at close hand the opportunities and amenities available to others but denied to yourself. The rural poor still tend to accept their status uncomplainingly; out of fear, habit, or resignation, they generally acquiesce to social arrangements under which they are the last to benefit.

In the broadest terms the poor of New York may be divided into those who support themselves and their families by gainful employment, and those who do not. The former consist of single or married men and women, most of whom head or belong to stable families and hold one of the low-wage jobs that continue to undergird the city's economy. New York has several hundred thousand parking lot attendants, hospital employees, restaurant workers, laundry employees, building custodians, and factory workers who try to support whole households on a minimum wage. Even with a low-rent apartment, raising a family on less than $8,000 or $9,000 a year means few diversions beyond daily necessities. Most of what New York has to offer is well beyond the budget of this class. Except for excursions to work, its members spend most of their lives in their neighborhoods. Given the constrictions within which they subsist, they could just as well live in Toledo or Tacoma. It has been argued that low-income areas often display an exuberance unknown in more sedate sections of the city, that the very theater of the streets provides continual excitement and entertainment. Even so, few familiar with this drama are satisfied with their status, and they show every sign of wishing to experience more of the world that now excludes them economically.

In 1972 the Bureau of Labor Statistics cited $7,578 as the income necessary to maintain a family of four on a "lower living standard" in New York City. It is difficult to contend that a household should be made to subsist on less than that figure. Establishing even that minimum, though, would automatically raise the price of hospital care, restaurant meals, building maintenance, and laundry services, not to mention supermarket bills and the dwindling number of domestic servants. Subway and bus fares continually rise because employees in those facilities have the power to exact wage increases for themselves. Hospital costs have also skyrocketed, even if wage gains by their employees have lagged behind other areas. New Yorkers who are progressive in persuasion protest the increasing cost of transit tokens and hospital rooms. Do they really want to do away with underpaid labor in all other sectors of the city? If this is what they mean, then they must face the prospect of experiencing fewer enjoyments than those now within their range. A family that can currently count on dining out several times a month will have to eat at home more often if busboys and kitchen porters are to receive $7,578 a year or its most recent equivalent. Whether they face up to this fact or not, New Yorkers of all ideologies have become accustomed to living off an economy built on cheap labor.

One suggestion has been that public funds augment the earnings of those in low-wage occupations. Yet none of the plans come near bringing families up to a $7,578 minimum, because subsidies on this order would impose markedly higher taxes on citizens irked with the burdens they already bear. To suggest that corporations and the very rich be taxed more evades the issue— middle-income families would still have to provide most of these costs. "To get a radical improvement in the income share of the bottom fifth of American families would require shifting income not only from the 5 percent of families with incomes above $25,000, but would also necessitate taking from those above $15,000."[2]

Furthermore, the major military outlay of the past decade has been not the Vietnam war but rather maintaining a costly complex of weapons and manpower, most of it nowhere near Asia. If proponents of income redistribution favor a Danish-style defense budget of, say, $15 billion, then they should say so explicitly. In addition, a lot has been said about the capacity of the American economy to create more jobs or at least to qualify individuals for positions currently available. Yet it is by no means self-evident that this economy can, in fact, produce gainful employment for everyone seeking a job. In any event, in New York City white-collar vacancies number only in the tens of thousands, while 10 times that number now occupy low-wage positions.

Even if all such persons underwent "training," New York could still create new occupations for only a minor fraction of its poorly paid.

It may also be argued that New York's culture and character bears a direct relation to its economic inequities. If wage minimums were to rise appreciably, the classes that now sustain many of New York's most characteristic amenities would end up holding a smaller share of the city's purchasing power. If people who now earn $4,500 were raised to $7,500, the expenditures and activities they would add to their budget of experiences would differ quite markedly from those that households descending from $30,000 to $20,000 would have to give up. Were New York's now comfortable classes forced to curtail their outlays, enough money would not be available to support Lincoln Center, Saks Fifth Avenue, La Côte Basque, Martha's Vineyard, the Dalton School, along with art galleries, wine merchants, bookstores, and other enterprises with well-off clienteles. Few households rising from $4,500 to $7,500 would spend their added income on these activities. If civilization depends on having a fair-sized class of consumers to nourish the artifacts of culture, then redistribution of wealth would produce blander and less adventurous patterns of consumption. The perplexity is hardly a new one: equality and justice on one side, and culture and civilization on the other. At this point the wealth of New York sustains some of the best French chefs on this continent, while that maldistribution keeps other families in tenements where their children risk lead poisoning.

THE UNPRODUCTIVE POOR

Over half of New York's low-income citizens are neither gainfully employed nor belong to families housing a wage earner. This part of the population does not contribute to the productive process, but instead receives its livelihood, either directly or indirectly, from the earnings of others. Tens of millions of non-working wives and children throughout the country are also nonproductive, but the difference is that they depend on husbands or fathers instead of other sources. Moreover, many of the city's well-to-do have incomes from securities which they did not accumulate by their own efforts, but rather, inherited. In fact, most New Yorkers exist in a condition of dependency; only 40 percent of the city's population receive wages or salaries in return for their services. The dependent poor differ only in that they usually have to live on less; in addition, how they spend their allowances is scrutinized more sharply.

In general terms the city's nonproductive poor may be placed in three broad and occasionally overlapping categories: (1) members of the households on the welfare rolls, commonly consisting of a mother and several children; (2) members of what may be called the city's criminal class; or (3) the aged or retired segment of the citizenry. Once again, a comprehensive analysis will not be attempted here, but rather some observations will seek to supplement the material found in standard commentaries.

At the end of 1972 the city's welfare population totaled 1,267,292, or approximately one out of every six New Yorkers. Of this number, 186,659 were disabled, blind, or the recipients of old-age assistance benefits, the latter program either supplementing Social Security checks of the elderly or for people without that coverage. Another 159,258 persons received "home relief" —cash payments for families whose earnings fall below a certain figure. These households consisted of 91,075 adults and 68,183 children. This left the largest single group on welfare, the 905,190 New Yorkers benefiting from stipends under the Aid to Dependent Children programs; here the recipients are 641,310 children and the 263,880 parents taking care of them.[3]

A closer examination of these statistics shows that alluding to "one out of six" gives only a partial account of the welfare situation. The welfare population consists of 354,955 parents, 186,659 other adults, and 709,493 children. Over 55 percent of the register is made up of schoolage or younger children. This preponderance of children means that less than 10 percent of New York's employment-age adults are on welfare, and most of these are mothers. But these figures also go beyond the "one in six" designation, in that they reveal that the 709,493 children on welfare amount to 32 percent of New York's boys and girls under the age of 18, or every third child in the city. This statistic is the most noteworthy finding in this breakdown and the most legitimate cause for concern.

Enough has been said elsewhere about the effects of the

welfare experience. It is not a pleasant way to live. In 1971, following a 10 percent cut from preceding years' levels, welfare allowances came to stipends of $2,124 for a family of two, $2,704 for three people, and $3,225 for a household of four. (These sums are not taxable, and the city also pays the family's rent, which averages about $1,500 a year.) The real tragedy is that few children raised in such settings get the chance to develop more than a fraction of their potential.

One of the guarantees of a free society is the right to produce children. Despite laws banning bastardy and fornication, and notwithstanding statutes specifying age of consent, in practice any two postpubescent Americans of different sexes can engage in the enterprise of producing a baby. If our population's growth shows signs of tapering off, it is due less to legislative inducements than to individual decisions abetted by more effective means of birth-prevention. Aside from the issue of whether the United States should have fewer people for ecological reasons, it would be well to consider the consequences of procreation at more personal levels. From the parents' point of view it is legitimate to ask how many of the children currently being born were originally intended and are actually wanted. It should also be asked whether some mothers and fathers, after several years of retrospection, regret having had as many offspring as they did? How many children enter and experience life in circumstances that enable them to enjoy some modicum of what this world and their own capacities have to offer?

The more than 700,000 New York children on welfare clearly stir such questions. All children receive some social subventions, and it may well be that boys and girls graduating from a suburban high school and going on to a state university have more public funds spent on their behalf than those raised on welfare. Middle-class use of the nation's resources may, in fact, cause more deterioration to society than lower-class vandalism or violence. But the issue with welfare is not what it costs the taxpayers, but the toll it takes on those enmeshed in that system. The issue is not whether the poor are having "too many" children; rather, it is how many of the city's youngsters on welfare were actually desired by their parents in the first place or were conceived under circumstances in which both the father and mother failed to contemplate the consequences of the sexual act?

None of the comments that follow should be construed as a plea for puritanism or nostalgia for a less sexualized era. Nor is any suggestion intended that the poor should show more sexual forbearance than other classes. At the same time, we do know that lower-class sexual intercourse results in more pregnancies and that more of those pregnancies eventuate in births. There is no substantial evidence that the poor plan for or welcome all of these conceptions. Much has been made of the notion that black and Puerto Rican men seek to prove their virility by fertilizing their partners. Perhaps. But most black and Puerto Rican women seem less than overjoyed at the prospect of continual pregnancies.[4]

Some evidence exists on this score. Beginning in the mid-1960s, clinics, health agencies, and city hospitals began distributing birth control information and equipment, particularly to married women who had already had at least one child. During the 12 months of 1964, before that program began in earnest, nearly one out of every five women on the welfare rolls gave birth to a child; by 1970 less than one in nine did.[5] This change is remarkable in a period of only six years. The rapid rate of decline suggests that these women welcomed the opportunity to avoid having more children. After all, it is almost impossible to compel a woman to use a contraceptive, and New York has never threatened to cut off anyone's welfare payments because of excessive procreation. Unquestionably, New York's reformed abortion statute also contributed to the decline in births. During the first full year under that law, over 80,000 residents of the city had pregnancies terminated. Approximately a third of these operations were paid for under the Medicaid program, presumably for women receiving welfare or earning very low wages. If both the abortion law and Medicaid assistance remain operative, it seems likely that even more low-income women will avail themselves of abortions.

But these are just beginnings. The city contains thousands of men, many still adolescents, who make no effort to have safeguards on hand as they make their advances to girls and women similarly unshielded. These exercises in irresponsibility are commonplace among those still in their teens, where genital

development runs ahead of a capacity for reckoning the results
of unsheathed sex. Sixteen-year-old girls end up rearing babies by
themselves, for the youth who did the fathering is often unwilling
or unable to undertake matrimony. Other infants are legally born
within wedlock, for most girls do eventually get married, including those who earlier had illegitimate offspring. But too many
partners in these marriages carry on with uncontracepted coition,
not always pausing to wonder whether the husband can support
so fecund a household. If he deserts his brood, finding them too
heavy a burden for his earnings, the wife may continue being
sexually active with subsequent partners who are similarly reckless
about the prospect of impregnation.

Of these progenitors, one observer asked, "where are these
men? Who permitted them to blithely disregard the most elementary responsibility of paternity?"[6] The answer is known by
those who look for such fathers in an attempt to serve them with
court orders for child support. As often as not, the search is for

> . . . men who scrabble through the social underbrush where the streets
> seldom have address numbers, let alone doorbells and welcome mats, and
> where the objects of the quest sometimes are off looking for low-wage
> pickup jobs, or nodding on drugs or wine, or standing idly on the streets
> with colleagues spinning out their lives in disbelief that there is any
> opportunity in it for them.[7]

Locating the fathers is not difficult for someone versed in the
sociology of the streets. The question is whether they can head
a household or, failing that, even provide support payments.

If young men used to marry the girls they impregnated, and
if husbands were more likely to remain with their wives, this was
because such duties were imposed by local sentiment and community pressure. New York's neighborhoods may have once comprised such communities, but the controls on which they were
founded have eroded in recent years. We can no longer argue for
a return to prenuptial abstinence. The release of sexual emotions
and energies is part of the way we live now; there can be no going
back to the sublimations of earlier eras. New York is having to
face the fact that several million of its citizens have in their loins
the capacity for creating life. Given that the city can provide only
a finite number of jobs, homes, and opportunities, curtailing
population even before conception seems the best place to begin.

Despite greater use of birth control by women and the increased availability of abortions, one out of every six children born in the city in 1971 belonged to a family on welfare, and almost a third of all New York's children end up on those rolls.[8] (In addition, 7 out of 10 of 1970's welfare births were out of wedlock.) Only a few agencies are prepared to offer contraception to young teenaged girls who, if not so protected, are likely to enter motherhood while still in their high school years. New York may be a sophisticated city, but the notion persists that armoring tenth graders against impregnation will propel them into promiscuity.

Most middle-aged New Yorkers are uneasy about the prospect of having their daughters of 14, 15, or 16 given contraceptive equipment. The city has a few private programs such as the Margaret Sanger Bureau's Teen Center, but they primarily attract middle-class adolescents who come without their parents' knowledge. A great deal of puritanism remains, even in progressive parts of the city. New York is not yet near the time when high schools or other local agencies will publicize their facilities for birth control instruction and equipment. The very image of midteen youngsters enjoying themselves sexually is not one that most adult New Yorkers prefer to contemplate.

THE CRIMINAL CLASS

When people speak of crime in the city, they mean street crime and particularly robbery. (The phrase *street crime* is a misnomer in New York; most robberies now occur inside, in hallways, elevators, shops, and subways. A person is much safer out on the sidewalk.) In all probability, muggers take much less from individuals than do corporate, syndicate, and white-collar criminals. Many executives swindle more on their taxes and expense accounts than the average addict steals in a year. Unfortunately concentrating on street crime provides yet another opportunity for picking on the poor. It is a scandal that a bank embezzler gets six months while a holdup man is sentenced to five years. And it is not entirely their difference in social class that produces this discrimination.

A face-to-face threat of bodily harm or possibly violent death is so terrifying for most people that the $20 or so stolen in a typical mugging must be multiplied many times if comparisons with other offenses are to be made. It seems likely that most city-dwellers would accept a deal in which they would not be mugged for a year if, in return, they allowed white-collar crime to unobtrusively take an extra 10 percent of their incomes. Everyone is annoyed by corporate thievery which drives up prices, but the kind of dread induced by thuggery has no dollar equivalent, or if it does, it is an extremely high one.

How pervasive is street crime? There are more than enough New Yorkers prepared to attest that "almost everyone on this block has been held up at least once." But there is only one set of official statistics. During 1972 citizens reported a total of 78,202 robberies to the police. The immediate reply, of course, is that some robberies—perhaps most—are not reported to the authorities. This may be so. Nevertheless, it is impossible to ascertain whether reported crimes represent half, a tenth, or a twentieth of the criminal iceberg. Sydney Cooper, former Chief of Inspectional Services in the New York Police Department, who has kept track of various studies for the RAND Institute's research on the city, suspects that there are, at most, about three unreported robberies for every one reported to the police. In his experience, middle-class victims tend to turn in a report, while most nonreporting individuals will be poor and disillusioned about any improvement in their safety. Given Cooper's calculations, about 300,000 robberies took place in New York in 1972. The city has close to 7 million residents, ranging from junior high school students to the very elderly, which means that each New Yorker stands the chance of being robbed once every 22 years. While the odds are clearly greater in the South Bronx, the Lower East Side, and Bedford–Stuyvesant, ironically the most noise about crime comes from Parkchester, Bay Ridge, and Staten Island, where the likelihood of being held up in an average lifetime is almost nil.

Even the most confident experts refuse to hazard a guess about how many people commit most of New York's robberies. Every large city contains a stratum of people who may be called its criminal class. Estimating its size depends on a string of suppositions, none of which can be grounded on reliable data.

Until recently, police officials have asserted that half of all the city's robberies were commited by addicts. (In fact, there is reason to believe that addicts prefer burglary and shoplifting.) In New York this would mean they are responsible for about 150,000 such crimes in recent years. This may sound plausible until it is recalled that the average addict may need about $50 a week to support his habit and perhaps another $50 for food and other expenses. Suppose that he can obtain this sum, or merchandise that will yield its equivalent, with one robbery a week and a few burglaries on the side. This means that if a typical addict performs about 50 holdups a year, it takes only 3,000 addicts to account for the 150,000 robberies attributed to persons on drugs. This total seems a trifle odd, since the head of the police department's narcotics division was still talking in 1973 about the city's having 200,000 drug addicts. Even the *New York Times'* specialist on the question wrote at that time that "there are 150,000 to 300,000 heroin addicts and users in the city, according to prevailing estimates."[9]

What seems to emerge is that the number of addicts who commit robberies is a very small proportion of the total. Apparently many addicts raise their cash by selling drugs to one another and by noncriminal means, including legitimate work. It appears that most "addicts" or "users" can actually take it or leave it alone and do not want or need a dose every day. Reducing the incidence of addiction would obviously cut down the level of crime, but slavery to a drug habit is not the major cause of holdups, especially if an analysis is made of the reasons for robberies carried out by people who are not addicted. In any event, it does not take many thugs to terrorize a city the size of New York. In all likelihood they number well under 10,000; even this figure would include those who embark on only three or four holdups a year.

No one knows how much better job the police might be doing. Cities have no choice but to accept the premise that a uniformed policeman pounding a beat or patrolling in a car deters would-be robbers. Hence the demand that the number of men on patrol, particularly on foot, be substantially increased. But no one is willing to predict how many fewer robberies the city might have if were there a police officer on every corner. (In 1969 the department estimated that such a deployment would cost $2.5 billion a year.) In theory, the presence of the police makes a potential criminal realize the high odds of his being caught. Unfortunately the deterrent value of omnipresent policemen cannot be gauged. The President's Commission on Law Enforcement and the Administration of Justice estimated in 1967 that the chance of a patrolman's happening on a robbery while it is actually taking place is about once in 14 years. Perhaps some sympathy should be extended to police commanders who have to decide which portions of their force they will assign to walking beats, riding patrol cars, and staking out likely locations in plain clothes. A good case could be made for putting the entire force in mufti and letting them wander unrecognized throughout the city. But how many taxpayers would be willing to give up even an infrequent glimpse of a blue uniform?

If prevention remains moot, the alternative must be apprehension. Catch those who have committed crimes—that is what plainclothesmen do best—and put them where they will not be able to harm their fellow citizens for some time to come. This is not the place to consider the question whether prison terms can ever rehabilitate criminals or even whether such punishment can discourage subsequent lawbreaking. It is simply noted that in 1973 New York State's prisons had fewer than 22,000 beds in less than ideal institutions where the annual cost of keeping an inmate was $6,000. At this point the focus will be on how the police go about catching criminals, which, after all, is one of their jobs, whatever happens further along in the judicial process. In 1972 New York's police force of about 30,000 men and women made 19,227 robbery arrests. The average police officer goes a full year without making an arrest. Compared with the figure of 300,000 robberies, a record of 19,227 arrests is a less than auspicious ratio.

But like other statistics, arrest figures are tricky. To begin with, 19,227 robbery arrests signify the number of *times* that policemen charged citizens. Contained in those 19,227 arrests may be only 5,000 or 10,000 or so people, some of whom were arrested two or more times during the year. The police department says it does not have the resources to keep track of how many people are arrested each year. If two or more people are arrested for performing a single robbery, each person is recorded as a separate arrest. Then again, at least some of those arrested for robbery are, in fact, innocent of any such crime. The police have been known to bring in the wrong man who may even plead guilty on a reduced charge out of despair of ever establishing his innocence. At the same time, many of the persons represented in the 19,227 arrests may have committed robberies in addition to the one for which they were arrested.

It is strange that a police force the size of New York's cannot make more than 20,000 robbery arrests in a year. The response of the police is that they are doing their best in an impossible situation. In addition to the reported robberies, they had to deal with reports of 356,101 other crimes in 1972, ranging from 1,691 murders to 75,865 auto thefts. An average detective may find that on a given weekend 30 such reports can land in his lap. He can legitimately claim that he could solve a lot more robberies if he were able to give a full week to each incident, especially tramping the streets searching for informants. For example, modus operandi files are still kept, a holdover from the days when detectives had the leisure for detecting. If, on being questioned, the victim recalls that the man who held him up used a white-handled revolver, the police can compile a list and then produce mug shots of men who seem attached to that kind of weapon. But such a procedure takes time. There is reason to believe that in a large city like New York only murder cases are treated with a full investigation, including a wide search for witnesses and rounding up of suspects.

Yet it may be better to have no arrests at all than ones based on perfunctory investigations, which is something the police themselves acknowledge. Unlike civilian law-and-order buffs, the police still realize that a person can be arrested only for having committed a particular crime. Henry Gordon cannot be charged simply with "being a criminal." It is not enough to protest that everyone in his neighborhood "knows" that Gordon is an addict and that he supports his habit by stealing. The police can arrest Gordon only if he can be convincingly connected with a specific holdup. If householders demand of their precinct that something be done about Gordon, they will be told that the police cannot act until evidence is produced linking him with an actual crime. If this seems frightening or frustrating, it would be well to ponder the consequences of not permitting Gordon the presumption of innocence. Those demanding that the police lock up all the "known" muggers in the city have at least some obligation to outline their strategy for street-clearing and to show how they will ensure that innocent persons do not fall into their net.

No one really knows how many robberies can be attributed to drug addiction. There is the suspicion that even if most addicts shook off their habit, some would continue to steal for all or a substantial part of their living. Suppose that through methadone or some other treatment an addict manages to kick his craving for drugs; even suppose he can get heroin legally and cheaply, as in Great Britain. Nevertheless, he may still join the ranks of those who engage in robbery to get money for their food, rent, clothing, and other amenities. Many former addicts have found jobs and stopped committing criminal acts. Drug programs justify their existence even if they lead only a handful of their participants out of the nether world of stalking their fellow citizens. But the options open to a young man who has gone off heroin are not much different from what they were before he got hooked. The jobs available to him still mostly involve washing other people's dirty dishes, parking cars, mopping floors, or pushing hand trucks for a take-home wage of about $80 a week—in short, wearying and dead-end jobs. Most poor people resign themselves to a lifetime in such positions. Crime results from those who prefer theft.

When it is proposed that each American city now contains a *criminal class*, this refers to those of its citizens who have few misgivings, perhaps none at all, about stealing from other people. Their thefts differ from those of other dishonest persons in that they are prepared to scare the daylights out of their victims in face-to-face confrontations. (They can also be distinguished from professional killers whose homicides are largely intramural.) The "crime problem," as every city defines it, centers on the existence and exactions of this class, which consists chiefly of young men who are unwilling to work at the kind of jobs our economy offers them. More ominously, this is a violent class, with its members ready to traumatize anyone from old women to people of their own background and economic standing.

London, Paris, and America's large cities have all contained such a class in the past. Everyone has read of men who would without compunction slit your throat for a shilling and of neighborhoods where policemen would walk only in pairs or not at all. But that is supposed to be the history, now past, of slums which reduced humans to little better than beasts. By 1900 that period had passed for most cities, and certainly for New York. During the first five or six decades of this century America's cities were remarkably orderly, with little violent crime and safe streets in most lower-class neighborhoods. These were the generations in which most adult New Yorkers were raised, and their memory is one of relative tranquility. In fact that half-century or so now emerges as having been exceptional in urban history. Its placidity depended chiefly on the modest ambitions and self-estimates of the poorer citizens. European immigrants and arrivals from America's own rural reaches displayed the sense of duty and spirit of deference often associated with feudal retainers. Those days cannot be re-created.

Members of the criminal class need not engage in a lifetime of lawbreaking. The city has plenty of peaceful citizens who, in earlier incarnations, held up shopkeepers and taxicab drivers. The class has a continual supply of recruits. How often do we stop to wonder from what source 15-year-olds in the slums obtain their spending money? If their fathers bring home $80 a week or their mothers are on welfare, those adolescents must raise their own cash for clothing, records, and other entertainments. Not all do so by delivering groceries. Yet despite all the research into delinquency, no one can say why one brother turns to mugging and the other labors wearily in a laundry. It is too easy to intone that poverty causes crime. The poorest classes produce most of society's convicted criminals, but at the same time, the great majority of poor people lead honest lives. For them, poverty has not turned them to crime.

Upswings and downswings of the economy no longer show a significant relation to crime rates, so some skepticism should be directed at those who assert that New York must create more "job opportunities" if the city is to deal seriously with crime. It would be well to inquire just what kinds of jobs might induce the average hoodlum to abandon his current maraudings. If he rejects a stupefying job at $80 a week, will the offer of $125 move him to relinquish robbery? Or will it take closer to $175, which raises the question of the kind of work he could do that would merit such a salary. None of these questions is meant invidiously, but only to suggest that robbery is one way some Americans assert that they deserve better than their economy has offered them.

Nowadays members of the criminal class blend into the general population. At any given time, it is likely that at least a few of the young men the average New Yorker passes on the street or sees in the subway held up someone the night before. But which ones should be feared? Without knowing for sure, many citizens grow anxious at the sight of any young man with a certain appearance or bearing. (Such men tell out of their experience when, being on a self-service elevator, others will draw back on seeing them already there. Those who enter have their hearts pounding almost audibly until they get off the elevator.) Interestingly, one police method operates on the premise that the city contains a quota of persons who can be counted on to commit crimes. To discover who these potential perpetrators are, plainclothes policemen masquerade in various guises and shamble down deserted streets on the expectation that they will eventually be jumped. Fairly soon they usually are, at which point backup men dash in to help with the arrest. The rationale here is that had the decoy not been there, his assaulter would have attacked an innocent victim later that evening; thus the trap saved an actual citizen from a mugging and put a criminal behind bars, thus sparing the city from his depredations for a while.

If "law and order" has served as a euphemism for racist attitudes, then proposals that the police be unleashed have a somewhat more specific intention in mind. Most of New York's robbery victims, whether black or white, would probably settle for protection from the black segment of the criminal class. That is, both black and white residents of the city would be content to take their chances on falling prey to such white muggers as stalk the streets. One Harlem writer has said as much in attesting that the problem for him and his neighbors is that "we stand menaced by our kith and kin."[10]

According to the 1970 Census, New York has 187,146 black men between the ages of 15 and 29. The only efficient way to make a dent in street crime (and by this is meant simply getting the criminals off the streets) is to withdraw the constitutional presumption of innocence from these 187,146 citizens.[11] For within their number lurk most of the city's criminals. The entire stratum would have to endure harsh and humiliating treatment if the dangerous members are to be ferreted out. That is what is being said, or at least whispered, with increasing stridency by those beseeching the authorities to "do something."

Take the matter of weapons. Most robbers carry a gun, or at least a knife somewhat sharper than needed to cut string. Every patrolman now has the authority to stop and frisk any citizen he has cause to believe may be carrying a felonious item. But courts have tended to require that the officer be able to give a specific reason for conducting that frisking. Simply asserting that the individual looked "suspicious" is not enough. Many New Yorkers would like nothing better than to have the police stop various of their fellow citizens as a matter of routine and pat them down, perhaps several times a day. Those who advance such a proposal do not contemplate that they could be applied to businessmen's attaché cases or the handbags of middle-class housewives. The target, of course, is the pockets of those 187,146 young men who are statistically most suspect.

Such a procedure might well round up a substantial share of the city's illegal weapons, as well as provide an excuse for putting their bearers behind bars. These roundups, though, would have to be sweeping and indiscriminate. For example, black muggers and murderers seldom dress in rags. Most are indistinguishable from black Columbia students or Chase Manhattan trainees, so those subject to frequent friskings would include Nigerian United Nations delegates along with black ministers, schoolteachers, and writers.

Middle-aged slum-dwellers may live in terror of local muggers, but they also have sons of their own who, they realize, would be subject to roundups if police powers were made absolute. Black wives, mothers, and sisters have no overriding confidence in the ability of the police to distinguish a string-cutting knife from one intended for throats. Nor are any criminals currently being "coddled" if by that is meant that those arrested are given a chance to show that they did not commit the crime with which they have been charged. As matters now stand, innocent persons caught in the criminal-justice system plead guilty to a lesser charge as the only way of getting home. Some citizens find it plausible to assume that even if a defendent did not carry out the crime for which he was arrested, he "must have" broken the law at other times and hence deserves whatever punishment he gets. Such an argument becomes even more persuasive if the suspect "has a record." "The police view is quite simple," writes Morton Hunt; "anyone who has ever been convicted or even arrested, or about whom the police have ever heard any derogatory gossip, is likely to be guilty of some present criminal activity."[12] The very idea that someone may be regarded as the "sort of person" likely to have engaged in crime, in fact, suggests a willingness to imprison some innocent people in order to sweep up more of the city's real criminals. This readiness to presume guilt, rather than innocence, shows how desperate many people have become.

Put simply, the tougher the police get, the closer the city will come to imposing martial law on 187,146 of its citizens. Most of those young men are as law-abiding as the rest of their fellow citizens, or at least those in their age range. But for crime to experience a substantial reduction, all 187,146 of them would have to be treated as presumptive criminals, and some would end up in detention because they were wrongly identified or someone had suspicions about them. Perhaps these remarks are obvious and have no need of reiteration; however, code talk about crime needs continual deciphering. If New Yorkers have something in mind other than roundups based on race, they ought to say so.

The problem of "street crime" should be understood chiefly as one created by a criminal class of young men, a class New York is going to be living with for a long time. The major cause of such crime is not narcotics, as the city will discover once—or if—it gets every addict either unhooked or onto a substitute. From one standpoint the city should count itself fortunate that so small a part of its population has taken to theft. That so many individuals remain honest while being treated so stingily by society should be a source of both amazement and confidence.

THE ELDERLY

The 1970 Census found 947,878 elderly people in the city. They comprise the fastest-growing age group in its population. Between 1950 and 1970 the number of persons aged 65 or over increased by 57 percent, whereas the number of adults in their thirties, forties, and fifties declined during this period. In addition, New York has a higher ratio of elderly residents than any of America's 10 next largest cities.

Unfortunately the Census does not provide explicit information on the economic status of older New Yorkers. It confines its analysis to the part of the population living beneath the poverty line, which means only the poorest of the poor. According to the criteria used by the Census, 206,124 aged individuals (about 22 percent of the elderly) subsist below the poverty threshold. This formulation offers a far from realistic picture of what it means to be poor in a city like New York, in that all individuals receiving more than $34 a week and all couples with incomes exceeding $43 a week are not counted as poor. But even in 1970 a weekly income of $100 provided little more than a bleak subsistence. It would have been interesting to learn how many of the remaining 741,754 elderly persons had incomes above the "poverty ceiling" but still below, say, $100 a week. The Census published such information in 1960 but failed to do so in 1970. Therefore the following comments rely on more direct forms of observation, which suggest that very few of New York's elderly inhabitants have enough money for the amenities of middle-class life.

While many older people live in rent-controlled apartments or homes with paid-off mortgages, and while Medicare and reduced transit fares offer relief in vital areas, in most cases the incomes they receive permit little more than the barest necessities. Some of these individuals have always inhabited the city's lowest income reaches, so the poverty they now know is merely the final chapter in a lifetime of exigency. But most were at one time productive citizens, usually earning enough to afford the conventional comforts of their times. With the onset of retirement they therefore found themselves reduced to a subsistence existence, made all the more tragic by lack of forewarning.

At the beginning of 1972, 886,635 of the city's residents

were receiving Social Security old-age benefits. Some were widows and retired women who began to draw pensions when they were 62. More than 70 percent of the city's Social Security beneficiaries receive pensions based on their own earnings records. In other words, only 30 percent are wives, widows, or widowers whose coverage comes from their spouses. Of the 556,098 women receiving payments, 570 had once been members of the labor force themselves. The average New Yorker, then, has completed a lifetime of labor, and his entitlement to retirement benefits might be thought to bear some relation to the contributions made during his productive years. There are also retired people—for example, domestic workers—who were not covered by Social Security while they were employed. They must wait until they are 72 to receive pensions of their own. A 7- to 10–year penalty is thus imposed on those who worked in jobs that were not covered or who were not married to someone who was covered.

Most elderly New Yorkers do not receive the maximum Social Security pension, for during their working lives their earnings fell short of the limit toward which employers matched deductions. In 1960, for example, Social Security taxes were drawn from the first $4,800 of an individual's income, which, in effect, meant that those who received less than that amount that year were stated to receive less than the maximum pension upon their retirement. In 1960, as in preceding years, over half of the city's wage earners failed to accrue the maximum equity in their accounts. Middle-class employees get much more out of the Social Security system than do the poorly paid.

As 1972 began, the averaged retired worker in New York City who was covered by Social Security, received a weekly payment of $33.46 as his pension. With the 20 percent rise in benefits that Congress enacted later that year, the average pension rose to $40.15 per week. This amount is hardly an auspicious income, and it may be argued that Social Security has turned into a grand delusion. Certainly some kind of surprise is in store for anyone who approaches retirement without other sources of income.

It is far from easy to survive solely on Social Security. It is virtually impossible for a widow who never worked herself and

must depend on the residue of her husband's benefits. Unfortunately no figures exist on how much old people hold in savings
and securities. The only available information comes from a
national survey conducted by the Social Security Administration
in 1968, which found that the average retired household had
some source of income in addition to Social Security. Table 5.3
shows (in the first column) the percentage of families who have
income from various sources. These total to 213 percent, reflecting the various kinds of income received. The second column,
which adds up to 100 percent, gives the percentage of total
income of the aged obtained from these sources. For example,
while half of the elderly families have income from assets, those
proceeds still come to only 15 percent of the aggregate income
enjoyed by aged households. Interestingly, only 5 percent of the
total income of the elderly came from pension payments by
private employers. Perhaps most noteworthy of all, a mere 3
percent of the households received regular sums ("personal contributions") of any size from their own children, and those gifts
came to only 1 percent of the overall income of the nation's
retired families. [13]

Table 5.3. Income Sources of Retired Households

	Percentage of Households with Income from	Percentage of Total Household Income from
Social Security pensions	86%	34%
Earnings	27	29
Income from assets	50	15
Civil service pensions	10	7
Private employer pensions	12	5
Veterans benefits	10	3
Public assistance	12	4
Personal contributions	3	1
Other (including annuities)	3	2
	213%	100%

These are national, and not New York, figures. In 1971
fewer than 10 percent of all elderly New Yorkers received Old
Age Assistance benefits from the city, either as a way of supple-

menting inadequate pensions or because they had no pensions at all. There seems little doubt that many more elderly people than have applied are legally qualified for such programs. Between 1967 and 1971 the number of persons receiving Old Age Assistance payments rose from 48,439 to 79,383, which portends a rising rate of applications in the future.

If New York has forgotten any people, they are the aged. In many cases they lead listless and limited lives, with even the money for a daily newspaper or a reduced-rate bus ride beyond their means. Many spend their days sitting *alongside* (not *inside*) the city's parks and squares or even in the waiting rooms of the Port Authority bus terminal. Older New Yorkers are the easiest prey for the city's criminals, thus many lock themselves in their apartments except for occasional expeditions for groceries or other necessities. These are people who have been left behind, sometimes by their now-adult children, at least some of whom can afford European vacations and swimming pools at their suburban homes. Any suggestion that sons and daughters who have reached their thirties or forties should share a more generous portion of their income—perhaps 20 percent—with their aged parents will be shown to be "unrealistic" by those asked to be the donors. They prefer to persuade themselves that Social Security, Medicare, and a rent-controlled apartment, along with some supposed stocks or savings, provide mother and dad with all the comforts they need.[14]

Older New Yorkers constitute a subdued presence. While many of them vote, those ballots fail to bring benefits to the extent that electoral influence aids other groups. They eschew organized protests yet receive no recognition for their self-restraint. The stark fact emerges that the city has no need of its elderly. They would be better off in a smaller city such as Amsterdam or Jamestown or Ogdensburg, where prices are lower and more deference is displayed to advanced years.

New York's aged are not a "problem" for the city—and therein lies their own problem. While their condition of life may occasionally cause some qualms of conscience, nothing they do discommodes the routines of other residents. In suburbs and other cities the aged can at least make their presence known by voting against school budgets and local bond issues. New York offers no parallel vehicle of expression, relegating older residents to the lowest political priority. Most are products of generations which regard demonstrations as unseemly, which explains the rarity of their marches to City Hall or appearances before public sessions, let alone more strenuous displays of discontent. The city's younger and more vigorous generations offer little indication of any willingness to assist their aged neighbors much beyond the margins now provided. Unless older New Yorkers are willing to organize the kind of commotion that has become commonplace among parents, public employees, and people on welfare, they will have to put up with the ignominies they now suffer. New York acknowledges only the existence of people who withhold their services, threaten its safety, or disrupt the machinery with which the city conducts its daily business.

BETWEEN POOR AND PROSPEROUS

Poised between the city's poor and its prosperous are people of modest attainments and ambiguous aspirations. The 1970 Census showed 43 percent of New York's families as having incomes ranging from $7,000 to $15,000, a material standard that made them substantially better off than either they or their parents had been a generation earlier. But these economic gains have been insufficient to compensate for feelings of beleaguerment that working- and lower-middle-class citizens now experience in a city where persons like themselves no longer have pride of place. Unable to settle for the modest goals of their parents, yet deprived of the respect they regard as their due, more and more members of these classes see New York not as home ground but rather as enemy-occupied territory.

These New Yorkers sense that they have been left behind, that of all the city's inhabitants, they receive the least esteem and recognition. At the same time, it can no longer be claimed that they are "forgotten." During the Lindsay years increasing numbers of candidates and commentators rose to acknowledge their existence, offering exegesis for their angers and anxieties. For example:

> This guy has a large commitment to the work ethic and he feels threatened. He sees people making fun of the work ethic, and he's confused and angry as hell.

They see no programs directed at them or their kids. They see their taxes rising and neighborhood services getting worse. They see the intelligentsia on television depict them as bigots and backlashers. And they're furious.

They represent failures in the great American sweepstakes, in that they have been economically upgraded but still have not shared in the credit-card goodies of our culture.

They represent insecurity in many ways, and a great deal of nervousness about never having made it in their own country or in the United States.

They're insecure. They're worried someone's taking their jobs now. And they can only conceive that someone's being helped at their own expense.

He feels locked in. They're looking for leadership. They're frustrated. They're frightened.[15]

The current tendency is to characterize this class as being composed of "white ethnics," running the gamut from Italian construction workers and Irish firemen to Greek shopkeepers and Jewish schoolteachers. Yet the racial connotation here begs some serious questions. According to the 1970 Census, for example, no fewer than 222,387 black and Puerto Rican families in the city had earnings between $7,000 and $15,000, indicating that middle-income status is by no means confined to Caucasians. If anything, increasing numbers of black and Hispanic householders share the aggravations of being in the center. The fact is too often overlooked that being in the midsection of the economy can be a common denominator outweighing distinctions of race, religion, and national origin. While race and nationality play a crucial role in the public mentality and deserve attention as and where they are relevant, they should not be confused with conditions arising from other circumstances. Outlooks and life-styles in St. Albans and along Edgecombe Avenue have much in common with those in Bay Ridge and Co-op City.

What, then, do these New Yorkers want? Generally speaking, they seem comparatively satisfied with the values they hold and the activities that engage them. Few show any desire to read the *New York Times* or attend off-Broadway plays or pursue a more cosmopolitan existence. On the whole, their desires and demands can be easily listed. What is less apparent is whether New York City can satisfy these aspirations.

First, they want a lot more money. It is not simply that New York boasts the highest cost of living of any American city except Honolulu. The point is that the expectations set by the city's marketplace leave all but the well-to-do dissatisfied. Given price differentials, a $7,000 salary in Clinton, Iowa probably equals about $10,000 earned in New York. But the Clinton citizen with $7,000 is substantially better off because his income buys him a far larger share of what his city's emporiums have to offer. A New Yorker earning $10,000 is made much more aware of the things he cannot have.

This dissatisfaction gap becomes even greater as working-class and lower-middle-class citizens begin to see themselves as deserving a better deal from life. The sad fact, however, is that the city's economy is not able to create more better-paying positions. While Congressman Hugh Carey could claim that "the average working stiff is not asking for very much," the truth remains that the things he wants cost a lot more than he may realize. According to Carey:

> He wants a decent apartment, he wants a few beers on the weekend, he wants his kids to have decent clothes, he wants to go to a ballgame once in a while, and he would like to put a little money away so that his kids can have the education he could never afford. That's not asking a hell of a lot.[16]

Even if these are his only aspirations, they are not going to be fulfilled by adding a few thousand dollars to his present income. While ball games and beer may cost relatively little, new housing and higher education require tremendous outlays. Some of these wants could perhaps be satisfied through public programs rather than personal expenditures. Such steps seem unlikely, however, given the antipathy to higher taxes displayed by these very classes of citizens.

They also feel they have not been receiving their fair share of official attention. With the recent stress on alleviating poverty, it appears to them that local and federal funds and facilities go almost exclusively to neighborhoods other than their own. The

poor have become more assertive. While John Lindsay was mayor
the city's response seemed to suggest that public money was
being used to buy peace at any price. Television coverage, the
Daily News, and less formal channels of communication elabo-
rated on generous grants allocated to slum schools, poverty programs, community clinics, legal aid, and preferential hiring. A
person earning $9,000 came away with the impression that wel-
fare allowances and ancillary services put the poor a step ahead
of those who work hard, pay taxes, and ask for nothing.

But the lives of most low-income New Yorkers were not
substantially altered by poverty programs. The conditions the
poor experience continue to be far worse in all respects, compared
with those of steady wage earners, even if at one point in the early
1970s families on welfare received almost as much as the city's
postmen.[17] The presumption nevertheless persists that the poor
have taken custody of the public purse. Because so much
animosity moves in a downward direction, surprisingly little attention is paid to the amenities the city bestows on people who
are already affluent. Maintaining the Wollman skating rink and
the Riverside Park boat basin, providing lavish quarters for the
City University Graduate School and subventions for the Metropolitan Museum of Art are costly commitments. According to
traditional canons, subordinate classes should attack those more
privileged than themselves. Reducing services for the poor in
New York has attracted stronger support than cutting down
outlays for the rich.

Another demand is for more respect. For all the celebration
of the Silent Majority and Forgotten Americans, this is not the
era of the working and lower-middle classes. They have been left
behind by history or, more accurately, by those who tell us where
history has been moving. The current decades, particularly in
New York, have been a time to be young, facile, and attuned to
a fast-changing age. Working people were respected, or at least
romanticized, during the 1930s because they were seen as an
exploited proletariat deprived of life's decencies. Whether as
Steinbeck's migrants, Farrell's slum-dwellers, or Agee's yeomen,
they were endowed with virtues often assigned to the oppressed.
In graduating to a more prepossessing status, though, these
Americans have lost their historical role. The mantle has passed

to black militants, California farm laborers, and youthful protestors.

Their only remaining claims tend to be antedeluvian: they have been loyal and patriotic Americans, they work hard and obey the law. Yet a person's declaration that he works harder than others is difficult to validate. The great majority of New Yorkers put in a full day—at least by their own assessment. Office clerks may be seen socializing on company time, policemen have been known to catch 40 winks, and delays and divisions of labor give construction workers respites from their more arduous activities. The impression arises that most blue-collar and office work is not "hard" so much as it is dull and that this is the real cause for complaint. An individual cannot gain credit for holding a tedious job, so his claim must be to stringent exertion.

What can a city *do* to give these classes the respect they seek? Esteem is largely a matter of historical circumstance. In one age the gallant warrior, the high school quarterback, or the rough-hewn businessman will receive deference; in another, acclaim will fall on an ascetic theologian or an experimental sculptor. The working and lower-middle classes still command respect in the parts of the country that continue receptive to traditional modes of achievement. But New York no longer enjoys a state of truce in which all classes agree to respect one another's aptitudes and attainments. All commodities, whether wealth or safety or esteem, are in short supply. The civic arena holds more competitors than ever before, with each class convinced that it will survive only if its aspirations win a place of dominance in the city.

HOW IMPORTANT IS ETHNICITY?

Following a hiatus of several decades it has again become acceptable to identify individuals by their ethnic origins. Obviously occasions arise when a useful purpose may be served by describing someone by the color of his skin or his national heritage. Most New Yorkers have an awareness of their personal histories. They think of themselves as *being* black or Jewish, Greek or Puerto Rican, Chinese or perhaps even Anglo-Saxon. The city has newspapers, restaurants, and places of worship that

cater to specific ethnic constituencies. People with common
backgrounds continue to choose certain neighborhoods. All this
needs no elaboration, but several unexamined assumptions un-
derlie the ethnic emphasis. These premises deserve discussion.

Quite plainly, connotations of religion and immigrant origin
are at a substantial remove from those connected with color. The
circumstance of having a black or brown skin carries profounder
implications than any other characteristic. Having an Italian
name or wearing Hasidic garb may evoke discriminatory reactions. But if a white person puts on well-pressed clothes and
watches his pronunciation, he will encounter routine receptions
in most employment agencies or real estate offices.

New Yorkers react to one another in racial terms. Upon
hearing of a crime, the first question concerns the respective races
of the victim and the perpetrator. On learning that 50 children
are to be reassigned to a local school, the initial inquiry concerns
their racial composition. It might be argued that color, in and of
itself, is not the real concern of the questioners. To the minds of
white citizens, new arrivals of another race mean that a school
or neighborhood will become dirtier and more dangerous than
previously. But why not simply complain about the kinds of
people who cause those conditions, without allusions to their
race? Everyone knows that most black citizens are law-abiding
and interested in safeguarding their surroundings. Of course,
New York has classes of people whose presence creates problems
for everyone else. But the city would experience a lot less
acrimony if it were able to perceive those problems as class
tendencies rather than via racial references.

Every age has at least one preoccupation that eclipses all
others. For urban America, it has been race. Every chapter of
this book reflects that fascination. Beginning with the opening
portrayal of the city's population and continuing into the analysis
of elections and birthrates and crime, facts and feelings about
color end up playing a crucial role. Even I have come to feel that
so many references to race seem an irrational distraction, especially when variations in wealth, outlook, and living styles cleave
the city in more important ways. At the same time, no theory has
thus far succeeded in delineating the roles that race and class play
in the lives of individuals and the life of a city. The best a writer

can do is give the reasons for his own feelings of intellectual helplessness.

There is no prima facie explanation why people need to refer to one another by race. Human variations only begin to evoke interest because someone finds it worthwhile to invest them with a more than routine importance. The initial fact of anatomical dissimilarities leads to a whole series of discriminations in which one gender profits at the expense of the other. People have a tendency to put differences to their own advantage by expanding the significance of human variations even when those exaggerations lack any reasonable justification. (A minority of the population have earlobes that are joined to their jawbones rather than wobbling free. It is not entirely Swiftian to imagine a society in which citizens with attached lobes would always be relegated to the end of any queue.) Certainly everyone would be happier if we ceased noting the color of people's skins. We cannot stop ourselves from actually detecting that difference, but we might register it in a neutral way without reading anything further into the fact (as we currently do with earlobes).

Under such conditions a book might be written without any allusion to race. But under current circumstances, a refusal to mention color would be a self-indulgence no author could afford, a moral exercise for private reveries, but hardly a realistic way to describe a city. New Yorkers think and feel and act and react as if race was the critical demarcation in their city's life. The color of one's skin has importance in New York just as the date of one's birth affects his status in Japan or his religion became a matter of life or death in Hitler's Germany. Whether due to stupidity, selfishness, or a combination of reasons, people distort the reality around them, imparting an unwarranted importance to trivial differences. We cannot ignore this behavior, no matter how irrational its expression. If people insist on stressing an attribute, then, that emphasis will itself have real consequences.

Suppose, however, that analysis leads to the conclusion that class lines in fact outweigh race in determining the character of a city. If the citizens themselves prefer to overlook considerations of class and concentrate instead on color, an author can only aver that he perceives a reality that seems to have escaped most other people. He could assert that New Yorkers will never understand

addiction or crime until they cease stressing the racial origins of
those engaging in such behavior. Given the structure of the city's
economy and the role New York plays as a receiving bin for the
country, it would still have such a class even if all of its residents
were precisely the same color. (Of course, in a juster society,
poverty would be distributed equitably among the races.)

It seems terribly detached to talk about criminals, welfare
families, and public school pupils without alluding to the color
of the people involved. The answer is that we must repeat such
references so long as New Yorkers themselves insist on conducting their own conversations in racial overtones. To demand more
dispassionate analysis is to forget that New York is not a laboratory and that its citizens are not participants in a sociology semi-
nar. If white residents act according to stereotypes, it is because
they prefer playing it safe to a scholarly pursuit of truth. With
respect to everyday decisions, racism may be the most rational
response. Every New Yorker carries a computer in his head, and
race is probably the prime variable in its equations.

Imagine that you ring for the elevator in a large apartment
project and both cars happen to reach your floor at the same
moment. It turns out that each car already has a passenger. Both
contain young men dressed in much the same way. In one elevator the passenger is black; in the other he is white. You are
standing midway between the two cars. Which one do you
choose?

Of course the odds are overwhelming that neither young
man will take a knife to you. Even so, the chances are still higher
against one having criminal designs. Suppose the odds are two in
a million that the black man will attack you; that still makes them
twice as great as the one-in-a-million odds for his white counterpart.

Imbalances of wealth and opportunity have been characteristic of urban life throughout most of human history. Yet in the
vast majority of cities all residents were of a single race and shared
a common national origin. The contrast between Brownsville and
Park Avenue in New York of the 1970s differs little from the
chasm separating Whitechapel and Park Lane in London at the
turn of the century. It goes without saying that New Yorkers
would be less preoccupied with race were welfare families, com-

mon criminals, and below-grade readers more randomly distributed. But even if the city were to completely disregard color in apportioning opportunities, it would discover the true dimensions of the injustices now attributed to racial discrimination.

If this chapter has one purpose, it is to stress class differences within the city. The excursus above has shown the difficulties in conducting such a discussion. An observer may contend that an emphasis on race renders people impervious to more important things in their lives. Their very focus on that factor becomes part of the reality of the city, hence one cannot claim that race is unreal or even unimportant. Perhaps we should wait for future historians who will compare our preoccupation with color with similar obsessions in other cultures and centuries. For this reason an easier place to examine the implications of ethnicity is within the white population of the city, particularly given the revived attention being paid to religion and national origins.

How important are their ethnic identities in the lives of white New Yorkers? We know from choice of neighborhoods, circles of acquaintances, and adherence to religious rituals that being Jewish suffuses the overall life-style of many Jews. But for other Jews their Judaism may emerge as a marginal part of their experience when ranged alongside other activities and interests. While two persons may both say "I am a Jew," for one it will encompass much more of his total existence than it will for the other. (Which plays the greater role in the life of a Jewish homosexual—his Jewishness or his homosexuality?) The tendency to categorize the city by its ethnic components implies that race, religion, and country of ancestry are the most salient traits in the lives of the New Yorkers thus characterized.

As far as white ethnicity is concerned several observers have begun to question just how seriously national heritages should be taken. Alluding to Italian–Americans, John Faggi of Columbia University has pointed out that "many of them know very little about . . . the great Romano–Italian civilization." There is not much discussion of Dante in the Belmont section of the Bronx and hardly a profound attachment to Rossini in the Bensonhurst part of Brooklyn. "The Italian has become homogenized," Pietro di Donato has pointed out. "There are few things they enthuse over except football and baseball."[18] How many Irish–American householders in Queens' Woodside can quote five lines of Yeats, and how many in the Inwood enclave of upper Manhattan can recount one plot of O'Casey's? "There is a dimension of sadness, a pathetic failure about them, an estrangement from their original vitality," Dennis Clark has concluded.[19] The culture of these groups has more to do with habits of domestic life than with intellectual or artistic heritages. If ethnic organizations really seek to rediscover their traditions, it will be interesting to see how much dedication they will apply to this endeavor. An appreciation of Synge or Donatello or Heine calls for an unusual degree of self-discipline.

Ethnic characterizations serve as a convenient shorthand. As Nathan Glazer has written: "in New York City, whether we say 'blue-collar' or 'lower middle class' or 'homeowner,' or whether we say 'Italian' or 'Irish,' . . . we know we are talking about roughly the same people."[20] Glazer's comment explains all the generalizations about the "Jewish vote" and other expressions of ethnic voting. For example, just before the 1970 race for senator, a statewide survey conducted for the *New York Times* reported that "attitudes on candidates and issues were more sharply defined along ethnic and religious lines than among economic or geographical distinctions."[21] The survey discovered that majorities of Irish and Italians were tending in different directions from black and Jewish voters. Yet a closer reading of the returns disclosed, for example, that 40 percent of those describing themselves as Irish intended to vote for either the Jewish candidate (Richard Ottinger) or the Episcopal candidate (Charles Goodell), rather than the Catholic candidate (James Buckley). If as many as 4 out of 10 "Irish" voters show such an imperviousness to their ethnicity, drawing attention to origins takes us only a short way toward understanding their behavior.

The ethnic shorthand reveals itself as part of a general pluralist ideology which stresses the multiplicity of groups in a society. Pluralism has been America's answer to Marxism, implying that *class* cannot describe institutions or behavior in this country. Imputations of ethnicity raise the hope that if people think of themselves as, say, Polish–Americans or Swedish–Americans, they will maintain communities and cultures that will provide a bulwark against the impersonality of a mass society. But also implicit in this hope is the hint that so long as people think of themselves primarily in ethnic terms, they will reject any temptation to make class the fulcrum of their consciousness.

The preoccupation with ethnicity goes further astray, insofar as it diagnoses social problems in terms of nationality groups. In this vein Nicholas Pileggi has written:

> Italian families are reporting the highest white drug addiction rate in the city and, next to the Puerto Ricans, the highest dropout rate in the city's school system. It is in Italian neighborhoods . . . that welfare cases have increased by 16 percent in the last two years, as compared with a 10 percent rise in predominantly black and Puerto Rican neighborhoods.[22]

No sociological data has thus far been presented to demonstrate how having been raised in Italian–American (as opposed, say, to Greek) surroundings so handicaps an individual that he drops out of school, turns to drugs, or goes on welfare. The Mafia stereotype, by itself, cannot cause that much disability, or at least none greater than prejudices about Jewish assertiveness or Irish alcoholism. If some Italians have problems, it would be useful to know whether their ethnic upbringings contributed to those conditions. At this stage the connection is far from proven.

It may be said in reply that ethnic emphasis is not so much a sociological description as a political stratagem. Drug addiction and welfare dependency are not peculiarly "Italian" difficulties. It may be that the best way to secure assistance for those in need is by organizing along ethnic lines. While mobilization of this sort may turn out to be successful in getting help for some people, even though their problems are not inherently "ethnic," the question remains whether priorities should be decided according to who can make the loudest argument. To focus on "Jewish poverty" or "Italian underachievement" means that poor Protestants and educationally disadvantaged Hungarians will get less attention. Perhaps it is too much to ask that the city deploy its resources toward those in particular need, rather than by picking out ethnic pockets. Parceling out resources by race, religion, or national origin is not only wasteful, but it deters individuals from discovering conditions that they have in common. People who have been ill served by society can either scramble among themselves or recognize their shared interests. Ethnic fractionation simply postpones the latter realization.

Classes cut through ethnic categories, frequently producing

tensions that outweigh ancestral affinities. Milton Himmelfarb has written of the rise of a "Jewish class conflict" within the city, based partly on disparate opportunities but also on commitments to divergent values.[23] David Halberstam pursued a similar theme in contrasting the city's schoolteachers with the planners and professors consulted by the Ford Foundation:

> Shanker's people are middle-class teachers, the daughters of cab-drivers, the sons of tailors, the Jewish kids who did not quite get into the Ivy League schools. . . . Most of the Jews whom Bundy met were people who made it, people of the same origins, but who by their brilliance (and a little extra luck) had forged their way into a world he had known. . . . But thousands and thousands of others had stayed behind in their neighborhoods, many of these becoming public school teachers within the city system, fighting all the problems of a decaying city. . . . Bundy's Jews made salaries of $20,000 a year, often in public-service–oriented jobs, not really worrying about their salaries, knowing that if they wanted, they could always cash in on their excellence and . . . experience.[24]

Anyone who has taught in the city colleges is aware of the cultural divide separating undergraduates of Irish or Italian origins from their parents. (In 1972, for example, the great majority of my Queens College students supported George McGovern, while their parents voted for Richard Nixon.) Matthew Holden has estimated that approximately 30 percent of the country's black population consists of what he calls "working class respectables." "They believe in work, hate laziness, and feel superior to 'those welfare people,' just as does the white working class."[25] To presume that a black civil servant earning $20,000 a year has as much in common with a mugger, a chambermaid, or a janitor of his own race as he does with a white civil servant earning $20,000 a year is as much a racist assumption as any other generality based on accidents of origin.

But apart from mirroring the public consciousness, there seems little reason for so many allusions to the city's ethnic composition. Does it really matter whether or not New York will be "predominantly black and Hispanic by the mid-1980s"?[26] The most serious insights into a city depend on understanding its class structure and the outlooks of its constituents. The point is not whether white residents will become a minority, but what proportion of the emerging population will have middle-class incomes and cosmopolitan values. Preoccupation with color of skin and countries of ancestry is superficial sociology, makes poor public policy, and provides misleading forecasts for the future.

THE COSMOPOLITAN CONSTITUENCY

Not all New Yorkers like the city. Many have mixed feelings. But there are also those who have found that only in New York can they lead their lives to the fullest. Chicago, Atlanta, even San Francisco, cannot provide a similar experience. London, with its charm and civility, may be fine for visits or even extended interludes. But after a while one must come home. Commuting from the suburbs cannot be compared with living in the city. To their eyes and sensibilities, any place but New York simply lacks the variety, tempo, and pressure that give an edge to one's personality and impart excitement to everyday life.

These are the inveterate New Yorkers: people who do not mind the crowding, who are not unduly bothered by litter or graffiti, who manage not to obsess themselves with fear and foreboding. They freely acknowledge that the city is not necessarily a "nice place to live"; but, then, their value systems have higher priorities than *niceness*. They know that survival in New York demands some adeptness at self-preservation, and that process can abrade the personality in not-so-subtle ways. Still, they have learned to live alongside one another and on the whole prefer that challenge to the undemanding amiability encountered elsewhere. While other epithets might do equally well, these citizens may be called "cosmopolitan New Yorkers." New York's role as a complex of world centers is what has attracted them to and kept them in the city.

For the cosmopolitan New Yorker, shops in Denver and St. Louis lack range of choice; theaters in Minneapolis and Atlanta, dance groups in Phoenix and Pittsburgh, even Toledo's and Los Angeles' art galleries, all seem second best. The sheer size of New York's cosmopolitan class provides a clientele sufficiently large to support a wide variety of amenities, as well as comprising a pool from which demanding individuals can draw circles of kindred spirits. "I need seven or eight million people from whom to select my 70 or 80 friends," a confirmed New Yorker once remarked.[27]

Only a minority of the city's inhabitants belong to this category. Any attempt to estimate their number would be an abortive enterprise, for the tastes and traits that make up the cosmopolitan temper cannot be translated into quantifiable categories. While Manhattan has a higher proportion of people who fit the pattern, it would be a mistake to overlook similar spirits in other boroughs. An affinity for the urban life can be discovered at all levels of earnings and education and among all religions and races. Cosmopolitan sensations are more apt to be represented among residents who supported John Lindsay than among his detractors, among readers of the *New York Times* rather than the *Daily News,* and within the subscription lists of *New York* and the *New Yorker* or the *Village Voice* and the *New York Review of Books,* as opposed to the *Reader's Digest* or the *National Enquirer.* But not all cosmopolitan New Yorkers see themselves as readers or voters. Many adventuresome individuals have their home base in Harlem or the South Bronx. Others focus their lives on the sexual, criminal, or aesthetic diversions that only New York can offer. Yet in the final analysis the principal criterion of the cosmopolitan mentality is the affirmative desire to remain in the city even if income or occupation permit departure. Many New Yorkers feel trapped in the city and would move if given the opportunity; the cosmopolitan citizen remains voluntarily.

What distinguishes New York from other American cities is not its sheer primacy in numbers but rather its higher proportion of people with sophisticated tastes, liberal outlook, and open-minded approach to the perplexities of our times. Every American city has at least some people who share this mentality. (The movement that nominated George McGovern in 1972 showed the presence of those constituencies in every part of the country.) But apart from Boston and San Francisco, major metropolitan centers tend to be dominated by citizens with fairly orthodox interests. Consequently, persons having more latitudinarian opinions play little role in shaping the sensibility of a Dallas or a Milwaukee or a Seattle. Only in New York can its cosmopolitan portion exert at least equal authority in defining the total ambience of the city. Commuters and out-of-town visitors augment the clienteles for New York's galleries, theaters, restaurants, and specialty shops, in many cases providing the margins that keep those activities operating. *New York* magazine, for example, could not survive solely with its 120,173 in-city subscribers; its 65,642 suburban readers, plus another 86,536 elsewhere in the country, make it a profitable enterprise.[28] Even so, the number of suburbanites who travel to the city for cultural reasons is not all that prepossessing in light of their economic and educational levels. Westchester, Nassau, Suffolk, and the nearby New Jersey counties have approximately as many college graduates as does New York City; yet, according to a survey taken during the Lincoln Center Repertory Company's performances during December 1971 (one of the few such studies available), only 37 percent of the audiences were from the suburbs. Those surrounding counties have more families earning over $25,000 than do the five boroughs of New York, but only about a quarter of the Museum of Modern Art's membership lists consists of people with suburban addresses.

Many of the men who hold prominent positions in the city during the day depart for its outlying areas after sunset. Almost 100 of the country's 300 largest companies have their headquarters in Manhattan, but among the presiding officers of these firms, over three quarters have chosen to live outside the city. Corporate executives make their homes in such havens as Bronxville, Chappaqua, Red Bank, Montclair, and Short Hills, with the largest single clustering in Fairfield County. In 1971 the top men at Shell Oil, General Telephone and Electronics, Continental Can, Continental Oil, Kennecott Copper, Time Incorporated, and Mutual of New York lived in Darien. The presidents or board chairmen of Kraftco, Combustion Engineering, Pfizer, American Smelting and Refining, Ingersoll-Rand, Crane, North American Phillips, Bankers Trust, and F. W. Woolworth had their homes in Greenwich.

Few executives associated with corporate headquarters have any allegience to or affinity with New York. They identify primarily with the national networks their companies comprise, and as individuals, most have no particular attachment to the urban life. More often than not they were raised in small towns, attended state universities, and spend the greater part of their careers in medium-sized cities as plant managers or with regional offices.[29] For them, coming to New York means, not the chance to live amid the swirl of a large city, but the chance to occupy a preeminent office in their company. Considering that the typical corporation president no longer has children at home, educational considerations cannot account for their choosing to remain in the suburbs. The suspicion arises that proximity to a good golf course carries more weight than being close to Carnegie Hall. "I've had it with cocktail parties and the opera," remarked one executive in urging his company to quit the city.[30]

The way of life and living preferences of corporation families illustrate the growing divide between the city and its suburbs. It is increasingly possible to identify individuals in terms of their having either an urban or a suburban temperament. An increasing number of suburbanites are deciding that they can do without the activities and amenities of New York. By 1970, for example, sales in outlying branches of New York stores exceeded those of their parent locations. All sorts of reasons can be given for this reluctance to come into the city—parking problems, fear of robbery, babysitting expenses—but the overriding fact is that a growing quotient of suburban dwellers seem content to spend their lives on the urban fringe. Their tastes are not so demanding that they cannot be satisfied with the shopping centers, steak houses, and summer theaters close to their homes. In other words, even for the well off and better educated, the suburb is becoming more of a self-centered society than a connecting point to the central city.

Can anything be done to ensure that recruits for the cosmopolitan constituency will continue to remain in the city? Generally speaking, it seems unlikely that official action will have much effect. Cheaper housing will not become available in Manhattan, although adventuresome families may press on to Cobble Hill or Carroll Gardens. Whether they will find public education to their liking is more problematical. There are elementary schools in every borough where reading levels reach national norms, and the city still has high schools graduating pupils acceptable to Haverford and Harvard. The time of decision can come at the end of sixth grade, when children from a protected elementary school most move on to a larger junior high school, where most of their classmates come from surroundings less conducive to serious study. Private schools have become so expensive that they are an option only for a tiny fraction of even upper-income households. By 1971 seventh-grade tuition in the city's 60 nonreligious private schools averaged more than $2,000. A family earning $25,000, which desired such an education for two of its children, would have to devote a quarter of its after-tax income to school-ing. It is not surprising that private school enrollments totaled less than 35,000.[31]

The most interesting aspect of the expansion of the city's higher-income class has been the entry of young people into its ranks. The 1950 Census showed that only 3 percent of the city's single individuals—15,815 out of 655,445—earned over $7,000. By 1970 no less than 12 percent of the single persons—131,730 out of 986,566—had incomes exceeding $10,000, a figure which pretty much equaled $7,000 in purchasing power 20 years earlier. Put another way, the number of single individuals in the top income range rose eightfold in the two decades. Law firms, city agencies, and an entire host of other organizations now pay high starting salaries to young people and promote them at a much faster rate than in the past. This trend has created a new constituency of consumers, not only for material goods and services but also for ideas, entertainments, and cultural and political developments of the sort that keep a city alive.

The city, as it is now constituted, provides endless diversions for what is probably the freest generation the world has yet known. Their activities range from radical politics and swinging sex to the boutiques and bachelors' bars in all parts of the central city. New York has shared in the national and international phenomenon called "youth," a period now extending from post-pubescence through the arrival of the first child, beginning as early as 14 and reaching into the late twenties or even early thirties. In part, the change has been economic. Young people have more money to spend either from their own earnings or those of parents. But more important is their desire to lead lives of their own in places of their own choosing. In the past, adolescents (now an anachronistic epithet, for it implies acquiescent preparation for adulthood) remained close to home, seldom venturing beyond their neighborhoods. Now the objective is to have an apartment of one's own or at least one to share with others of your generation, with the surrounding city as territory for exploration. If secretaries, stewardesses, and novitiate stock-brokers fill the East Side's air-conditioned canyons, other young people settle for less commodious surroundings. Some of the most genuine "communities" the city possesses consist of young men and women who have come to share common political, intellectual, or even hallucinatory interests.

The growth of this constituency stems in part from the advent of the birth control pill and the availability of abortions, which have permitted young couples to postpone having children. This means that with both of them working, they stay in the city for an appreciably longer period than was formerly the case. In a growing number of instances single New Yorkers are putting off marriage until they are into their mid- or late twenties, for being unattached in the city is a lot more exciting than in earlier generations. Before the mid-1960s young people were apt to spend perhaps three or four years in New York until the arrival of children speeded them to the suburbs. With the postponement of pregnancies, such individuals may still inhabit the city as they approach or move into their thirties. This prolongation effectively doubles the size of the cohort, for one person spending eight years in the city equals two who remain for only four. And exemption from the burdens of childrearing permits these individuals to create lives for themselves that affect the entire atmosphere of New York.

The perpetuation of a cosmopolitan class will rest largely on its willingness to remain childless. For example, the city only remains viable if it can keep alive at night. In most American cities the central section becomes deserted at sundown as clerks and customers and other employees make their way to the suburbs. Downtown Cleveland, Detroit, and Houston turn into darkened chasms; downtown Chicago and Los Angeles show signs of activity, but people there drive directly to their destinations and seldom stroll the streets. New York remains about the only walker's city, and its survival depends on having citizens who are willing and able to spend their evenings in public places. In 1950, when the middle- and upper-income classes made up only a quarter of the population, New York families employed 88,370 domestic servants. Many of those maids lived in, freeing their employers for nocturnal activities. By 1970, with many more of its residents comfortably off, the city had only 39,979 domestic servants, the vast majority of them daytime help. Because of babysitting costs and the availability of television, the suspicion arises that parents today are more home-bound than were those a generation ago.

Citizens unencumbered with domestic duties have more income for the sort of expenditures and entertainments to be had in a cosmopolitan economy. The absence of offspring allows for flexibility in timetables, with a midweek evening able to run until 2:00 A.M. if the company proves congenial. One can always get by on a few hours' sleep and make it up the next night—provided there is no worry about relieving a babysitter at a specified hour. Young people, perhaps because they are lither of limb, seem willing to venture into parts of the city others see as depressing, dangerous, or too far from familiar tracks. Finally, as many eschew conventional careers and feel no need of approval for their appearances, they add both color and an air of informality to the city's landscape. Besides, small towns, suburbs, and the middle-sized cities of the United States can be counted on to provide more than enough children from the coming generations.

If suburbia's special character depends on tricycles and swingsets, the urban experience calls for adults having the freedom to define themselves amid the clutter and congestion of a cosmopolitan center.

6

Not Just Another City

"We Americans don't like our cities very much," John Lindsay said while he was mayor of New York.[1] Millions of Americans have expressed similar sentiments by the simple act of moving away, as often as not to the suburbs. Every successive Census shows a smaller portion of the population living in its urban centers. In 1950, 144 of every 1,000 Americans resided in one or another of the nation's 10 largest cities. By 1970 they could claim only 104 of every 1,000. Moreover, not all city-dwellers like being where they are. "Given a free choice," Joseph Lyford testified, "urban American is much more likely than not to move out of the city to a rural or semi-rural area."[2] A Gallup sampling late in 1972 supported this opinion, finding only 20 percent of the nation's city-dwellers prepared to list their location as their first choice.[3]

In this matter, as in others, New York differs from other cities. A survey conducted for the *New York Times* in 1974 reported that 54 percent of the New Yorkers they interviewed said that they stayed in the city because they wanted to, not out of economic necessity.[4] Even among those only mildly enthusiastic about New York (notably Puerto Ricans and blue-collar workers) at least 40 percent still made living in the city their first preference. There may be widespread disaffection in Cleveland or Baltimore. New York, however, can claim the loyalty of about half its inhabitants, no small proportion, considering the national opinion of urban life.

140

Even so, it would appear that almost half of all New Yorkers want to leave. Some already have plans underway; others cannot afford to move or are unsure of the reception they might receive elsewhere. As far as these families are concerned, it seems unlikely that many of them will change their minds. Personal safety will not increase in a measureable degree, a renaissance in the public schools is unlikely, and slums will continue spreading into neighborhoods previously considered stable.[5]

Many residents remark: "I would be happy to remain in New York, if only. . . ." They then go on to recite a list of conditions so exacting as to suggest that they would settle only for a city tailormade to their own design. The causes of crime, conflict, and living costs are chronic and well beyond the resources of even the most enlightened officials: "the most fundamental problem of the central cities . . . is of such a nature that it cannot be 'solved,' or even much relieved, by government action at any level."[6]

In addition, many individuals become troubled as they begin to detect some of the abrasiveness of the city in their own personalities. They wonder whether their share of New York's rewards compensates for the psychic price they are paying. Not everyone has the temperament for such a life, as Richard Whalen once pointed out in an elegiac passage:

> The fashionably tough-minded myth persists that the world's greatest city owes its inhabitants nothing, except the chance to grab the brass ring. Out of a kind of sad, proud stoicism, New Yorkers cling to this life to convince themselves that they are still in the running when they know they are not. It is the only consolation prize New York offers. The truth is that New Yorkers of humble talents and ambitions derive no benefits from living in the world's greatest city, but instead pay more for less with each passing year. They would be better off living in Cleveland, where at least they would not have to pretend that second-rate is best.[7]

One can live a New York life in many ways. Staten Island's more rustic reaches claim as rightful a status as the high-density apartments of mid-Manhattan. Many among those committed to the city choose a one- or two-family house at the outer edge of a residential borough. "Americans have clearly sought the suburban condition of living, often within the great cities themselves," as Daniel Elazar observed.[8] One can stroll through Eden-wald and Canarsie, or by Bayside and Eltingville and for a moment think oneself in a medium-sized Iowa city. Many Brooklyn shoppers journey to centers at the far end of their own borough rather than take the subway to Manhattan. No one has ever computed how many times each outer borough resident comes "into the city," but such a poll would find that large parts of the population make that trek only rarely.[9] This isolation has always been true. In 1939 an anonymous correspondent reminded his readers that New York contains many "people who, but for slight differences of custom and accent, might belong to Detroit or Pittsburgh or Memphis. . . . They do not crave, they are not particularly aware of, the vastness of the metropolis. In a general sense their lives are closed, their horizons contentedly bounded within a neighborhood; and they prefer to have them so."[10] Even now, in a more mobile and transient time, New York has many people who live in such a closed environment. They were born and raised in the city's neighborhoods and prefer that life to any other. Some have thought of moving—who hasn't contemplated California?—but concluded that New York gave them the life they wished to lead. That they have chosen to stay on affirms both their allegience to the city and their stake in the future.

Still, there is a problem. Their conception of the urban experience embraces few of the ideas and institutions that make New York a world capital. While New York may genuinely be their home, a congenial neighborhood in Minneapolis would give them more satisfaction than the impersonal apartments of Manhattan's East End Avenue. The question concerns which conception of New York's identity is to have priority.

Every city can claim a distinctive character. Each will point to traditions and tendencies they see as uniquely their own, certainly sufficient to distinguish them from other places. If these sensibilities deserve a certain deference, some perspective is also in order. For among America's cities, only New York stands alone. Philadelphia and Fort Worth, Boston and Chicago, even Los Angeles, take on much of a common coloration when set alongside New York.[11] New York's claim has always been that within its perimeter reside the nation's most interesting people. They are not necessarily the best-looking, the best behaved, or persons most Americans might want for their neighbors. But the very sensation of living in New York can bring out traits and talents that would remain dormant in less tumultuous settings.

In many ways the question underlying John Lindsay's bid for reelection in 1969 was whether New York should remain a cosmopolitan center or give priority to becoming a pleasanter place to live. Lindsay personified the former emphasis, while his two opponents asked, in so many words, why New York could not emulate an Indianapolis in providing efficient services and serene surroundings. Lindsay represented the position that New York was not simply another, somewhat larger, city. Rather, as one of New York's first citizens put it, it is "the greatest city in the world: the most magnificent, most creative, most extraordinary, most just, dazzling, bewildering, and balanced of cities."[12] If a citizen's priority goes to clean sidewalks, safe streets, and polite salesclerks, he should move to a place that is content to be safe, clean, polite—and not much more.

Other cities may feel they have done their duty if they finance a new stadium or renovate an old concert hall. New York has more varied responsibilities. It has an obligation, for example, to ensure that its sculptors have cheap and commodious studios, and it must do all it can to preserve its scholarly bookstores. It has architectural landmarks which must be kept standing even when they no longer serve a profitable purpose. In these and a thousand other ways, New York must remain a capital for tastes that a Houston or a Milwaukee could not conceive of accommodating. New York is an atmosphere and an idea. Its air of adventure and innovation serves the whole nation and infects the world. It would be tragic if disaffected residents in its own midst were to dismantle an edifice that has no equal on this globe.

The same forces that have made New York a more exciting city have also made it a more dangerous place to live. New York has a lower crime rate than a dozen other American cities, but few New Yorkers sleep more soundly upon learning that they are more likely to be robbed in Philadelphia or murdered in Detroit. Most tend to compare current conditions with the safety of past periods. New Yorkers of all classes have an expanded estimate of their worth and expect a greater share of what the world has to offer. These heightened self-estimates seem more endemic to

New York than other cities. Its citizens want more from life and are prepared to assert themselves to have that experience. Many have come to the city for just that purpose. For some, this means searching for an obscure Ibsen production in an old garment loft; for others it involves architectural explorations in the outer boroughs. For still others it may entail discovering a sublime cheesecake or an overlooked cabinetmaker.

Energy and imagination often express themselves in other ways. New York can boast the most flamboyant street gangs, the most brazen graffiti, and the most sophisticated pimps of any large city. Displays of the human spirit reflect variations in class and culture. Not every temperament can or will work within established institutions. The city offers few opportunities for skills which surface in the adornment of subway cars or managing a conglomerate of streetwalkers. Furthermore, people who bypass conventional careers no longer feel a sense of shame. Irving Kristol is a spokesman for those worried by these feelings of self-importance:

> These people will not be satisfied with a very slow, modest improvement of their condition, but insist that the improvement be substantial and swift. The previous immigrants to our cities would have thought such a demand presumptuous; they were resigned to poverty in their own life-time and placed their hopes for improvement with their children and grandchildren. This kind of resignation is going out of fashion everywhere in the world.[13]

Dickens and Balzac both understood that the excitement of a city cannot remain confined to its safest strata. Paris had its brothels, as well as its salons; London's great houses were a short ride from the most savage of slums. Bill Sikes and Monsieur Vautrin were as representative of their eras as Benjamin Disraeli or Honore de Balzac himself. Throughout history most great cities have had their share of violence.

Those nostalgic for a New York of an earlier era usually recall a safer, more placid, place which conducted its business with few signs of hostility or tension. For example, before World War II, the city's middle class was quite small. Its ambit of interests could be seen in the institutions it sustained. They ranged from the *Herald-Tribune* and *New York Sun* to Saks–34th

Street and Black, Starr, and Gorham. They included supporting the Brooklyn Museum, Lewisohn Stadium concerts, and functions at the Concourse Plaza. This class provided the major clientele for the city's theaters, its private colleges, and the apartment houses along Manhattan's Central Park West and Brooklyn's Prospect Park West. On the whole, they comprised a bourgeoisie, almost in the classical sense. They adhered to traditional values, led unadventuresome lives, and acknowledged their obligations to local culture.

Until fairly recently most New Yorkers belonged to the working class, admitting to that status throughout their lives. The city had fewer poor people, if that means individuals existing outside the regular work force. Jobs were available even for illiterates, and virtually everyone worked. Those who became Bowery derelicts or huddled in Hoovervilles kept to themselves and posed no public threat. In that past, New York had fewer families with only one parent; it had fewer truants and teenagers prepared to use violence; and addiction did not render large numbers of people unproductive. For at least the half-century from 1900 to 1950 an internalized discipline and obedience to authority made for a citywide consensus on property and privilege. New York cannot return to those days, nor should it seek to do so. The price of its placidity was a society in which most citizens were never permitted to develop their tastes and talents beyond the barest minimum.

Some scholars have taken the view that multimillion populations create so many problems as to outweigh any advantages of scale. "The all-around optimum size for a contemporary American city is probably somewhat between 50,000 and 200,000," observed Robert Dahl, one of the nation's most respected political scientists.[15] And in Lewis Mumford's view, "a city over 300,000 population ceases to have many of the most valuable attributes of a city."[16]

Yet anyone who has known cities of that range can testify to their constrictions. The optimums suggested by Dahl and Mumford, to take just the opening of the alphabet, would include Allentown and Altoona in Pennsylvania and Abilene and Amarillo in Texas. Yet cities of that size lack sufficient numbers to support any save the blandest of interests. An Abilene will not have enough customers to maintain a good French restaurant, while Amarillo does not have enough homosexuals to make that a congenial life for those who choose it. Allentown has too few numismatists to support a worthwhile coin store, and there are not enough film enthusiasts in Altoona to ensure that lesser-known movies reach its screens. If urban Americans were dispersed to cities in this range, they would have to abandon avocations of any unusual nature and settle for the common denominators that can be found in an Altoona: golf, childraising, and perhaps a local theater group. Most Americans do not have esoteric tastes. They do not yearn for special foods, sexual variations, or someplace where they can always find a chess game in the early hours of the morning. But there are people who have such leanings; for them, a cosmopolitan city is necessary.

Even New York's suburbs lack the major amenities present in the city itself. Perhaps if all of New York's suburbs were concentrated at a single compass point, then they would have large enough clienteles for a ballet company, a fine arts museum, and several Szechuan-style restaurants. But because the potential constituencies for such activities are scattered from Short Hills to Stamford and throughout Suffolk and Rockland counties, none of these enclaves has the numbers to sustain more than the basic country clubs, steak houses, and assorted drive-ins. The territory the Census calls the "New York–Northeastern Standard Consolidated Area" actually has more people in its eight-county fringe (8,283,838) than are in the five boroughs of the city (7,894,818). Furthermore, these suburbanites are better educated, have higher incomes, and work at more expansive occupations. Yet despite their credentials, the suburbs cannot produce amenities much different from those found around Kansas City.[17]

New York has need, most of all, for people who actually want to live in a crowded city, who do not mind—in fact like—being surrounded by strangers, who delight in its fads and fashions, its vitality and anonymity. A person does not have to be wealthy or well educated or even steadily employed to enjoy the city. Nor does everyone need to be especially creative. Most will serve as an audience, but it must be one attracted to experimentation and eager for new departures. A cosmopolitan city will be extraordinarily wasteful as well—of time and attention, of affections and ambitions, of human capital and material resources. It takes risks for the rest of the country, testing ideas and developing talents in ways impossible in a Denver or a Dallas. If New York is to retain its identity, to continue its contributions, it must have a plurality of citizens who live there by choice and affirm its special status.

This is not to imply that all others should be exiled. In fact, people unhappy with the city usually leave of their own accord once economic circumstances permit. A world capital cannot make family life its first order of business. Other settings gear themselves for that function, offering open spaces and successful schooling. The city's public schools will continue to deteriorate, partly because the majority of pupils come from surroundings inimical to sustained study and partly due to their being put in the custody of civil servants who commit little of their lives to the educational calling. Neighborhood New Yorkers will use the public schools as long as they can and alternatives as long as they exist. But even with new residential building, neighborhood New York cannot be expected to hold its own. Birthrates and age distributions in and of themselves guarantee its attrition.

A cosmopolitan city raises difficult questions of ultimate values. At this point New York subsidizes activities having comparatively prosperous clienteles. Admission charges for Lincoln Center productions, for example, are lower than otherwise, due to public aid toward the physical facilities. Should people earning $30,000 a year pay a few dollars less for opera tickets when slum children need decent clinics? Similarly, restaurants and other amenities rely on underpaid labor their patrons seldom see. The cuisines of Chinatown—one of the glories of New York—would disappear were it not for illegal aliens who wash dishes and haul garbage under conscienceless conditions. There is no answer to this dilemma. Every great city has exacted a human toll, whether to build its cathedrals or nourish its poets. In a more moral New York, where humanity had the highest priority, the well-off would pay their full way, with that cost including a fair wage for every service they employed. The consequence would be that once subsidies were withdrawn from persons at the $30,000 level, audiences for the opera and ballet would dwindle to a fraction of their current figures.

Civilization depends on subsidizing entertainment for a class that is already comfortable, just as it needs an exploited class to hold down the costs. We used to hear of finely stitched gowns over which seamstresses went blind. That equation has its counterparts in contemporary New York. If the city appears to show more compassion than it did in the past, it is evidenced mainly by wishfully thinking that there must be an economic formula that can subsidize all classes, with none the loser. A cosmopolitan outlook need not mean an end to self-interest.

Few cities in history have achieved greatness. Even fewer have kept that status for successive centuries. How long can New York's stature survive? The chief problem, of course, is employment. If people are to come to and stay in the city, jobs must be waiting for them. Over and above its decline in manufacturing fields, New York has been losing an average of 20,000 white-collar and service positions each year. Any local economy must provide something of value the outside world both wants and is willing to pay for. Books and magazines, music and art, advertising and financial services sold to the rest of the country, all bring in cash. But not enough. Not nearly enough, certainly, to provide employment for everyone wanting a New York life. In theory, the city could create more jobs, but in practice few of them would add enough value to justify their place on a payroll. Many of the services that used to emanate from New York are now supplied elsewhere. Each year the city comes on more strongly as a center of consumption while its productive counterweight grows lighter. Some kind of thinning will have to occur.

The eventual decline of New York does not mean another city will take its place. No such center looms on the horizon nor will any emerge. Rather the result will be scattered regions, each doing some things quite competently but without any particular pace or flair. Metropolitan Minneapolis and suburban San Jose give a glimpse of that post-urban world. New York has perhaps one more generation during which it can command preeminence. But not much more. Those who enjoy its life should make the most of it, for it can't last.

APPENDIX I—TABLES

Table I.1. Characteristics of Ethnic Groups—I

Age	Puerto Rican		Black		White		Total	
Under 30	537,423	14%	964,498	26%	2,229,791	60%	3,720,278	100%
30 to 64	252,738	8	615,704	19	2,357,535	73	3,226,706	100
65 and over	21,682	2	87,913	9	838,283	88	947,878	100
Total	811,843	10%	1,668,115	21%	5,414,904	69%	7,894,862	100%
Family Income								
over $15,000	8,991	2%	42,681	9%	433,752	89%	485,424	100%
$10,000–$15,000	25,796	5	76,690	15	402,136	80	504,622	100
$5,000–$10,000	78,253	12	151,660	24	409,973	64	639,886	100
under $5,000	87,636	20	123,873	29	217,502	51	429,001	100
Total families	200,676	10%	394,904	19%	1,463,363	71%	2,058,943	100%
Occupations								
managers and proprietors	7,538	3%	18,514	7%	224,140	90%	250,192	100%
professional and technical	9,704	2	58,183	11	434,285	87	502,172	100
clerical and sales	54,236	5	177,039	16	865,244	79	1,096,519	100
nonwhite collar	142,825	11	334,322	25	845,430	63	1,342,487	100
Total employed	214,303	7%	588,058	18%	2,389,009	75%	3,191,370	100%
Education								
attended college	12,030	1%	89,818	10%	787,566	88%	889,414	100%
completed high school	57,386	4	252,477	19	1,040,901	77	1,350,764	100
not complete high school	275,712	11	500,723	20	1,758,403	69	2,534,838	100
Total age 25 and over	345,128	7%	843,018	18%	3,586,718	75%	4,774,864	100%

APPENDIX II

The Census and the Cities

Unlike sample surveys, the United States Census remains the only poll that tries to question everyone. It also tries to avoid ambiguities. Words like *about* or *approximately* never sully its columns. The Census alone can unabashedly announce that 6,584 New Yorkers were born in Lithuania, that 49,744 families share toilet facilities with another household, and 297,132 of the city's residents walk to work.

But these numbers give only an appearance of precision. Some people fail to turn in their Census forms, and others evade being interviewed. In several instances the enumerators have been known to overlook whole rows of houses or apartments. Common sense also suggests that not all of a city's addicts, alcoholics, and illegal aliens end up in the tabulations. Unfortunately, there is no good way to find out the extent of the undercount. The safest recourse is to rely on the Census's figures as if they reflected reality, while at the same time retaining the right to raise an eyebrow if the statistics seem a bit awry.

For example, the tables for New York City in 1970 list 77,862 black women between the ages of 20 and 24 as living in the city but only 55,953 black men in that age range. That comes to 139 women for every 100 men. Some of the "missing" men were away from the city because of military service or prison sentences. A higher male mortality rate would account for another part of the gap. Still the suspicion remains that a lot of the men were around while the Census was being taken but avoided filling out the forms.

155

Another problem concerns the Census's decision to restrict itself to questions that can yield unambiguous answers. It would be nice to know that a city contains exactly 217,308 intellectuals or 159,077 homosexuals. However, it seems unlikely that the Census will satisfy our curiosity in such matters, for it prefers to avoid areas where we lack standard definitions.

For example, who is an "ethnic" American? The Census relies here on hard facts, not subjective impressions. If you were born abroad or if one of your parents were, then you are put down as "foreign stock" under the country of your or your parents' birth. (If your mother and father came from different places, you are assigned to your father's country.) Boston, for instance, has 51,716 residents who were born in Ireland or whose parents came from there. There are, of course, many third-generation Bostonians who consider themselves "Irish" or at least "Irish–Americans." We have no statistics on them, though, because the Census does not ask people where their grandparents were born. Because it prefers to play it safe by sticking to the first and second generations, the Census understates the number of "ethnic" Americans in Boston and everywhere else. At the same time, no one really expects the Census to ask people "do you feel Greek?" All in all, it is happiest with responses which can be arranged in neat columns and uncontroversial categories.

Do people tell the truth to the Census? There is probably quite a bit of fibbing about age, time spent in school, even marital status, yet it seems unlikely that these inaccuracies affect the totals by more than a few percentage points.

From time to time an opportunity arises for one to run a check. For example, the Census always asks each family to state its income. The figures New Yorkers reported in 1970 added up to $29,374,366,000. According to the Internal Revenue Service, income tax returns from New York for that same year gave a total adjusted gross income of $28,039,145,000. This makes a surprisingly close fit, or at least one that ought to satisfy skeptics. (If people do lie about their incomes, they apparently tell much the same story to both the Census taker and the tax collector.)

While the Census publishes a great deal of information about the cities, it provides its readers with only the most minimal guidelines when it comes to unearthing and interpreting those statistics. What will follow here, then, is an informal inventory of what the Census has available specifically on the cities. All of the tables that will be alluded to appear in compendium volumes, covering either an entire state or country. A state volume, for example, will have tables for its counties, rural populations, and the state as a whole, as well as figures for its cities. The Census does not have any report which brings together all its material on, say, Chicago. As will become apparent, anyone interested in Chicago or any other single city will have to inspect a wide spectrum of publications, and in some cases a volume may have only one or two pages on the city in which you are interested. So it is best to browse before buying.

WHAT THE CENSUS TELLS

Census routines may sometimes seem arbitrary and even a trifle eccentric. Everyone who uses the reports finds himself disagreeing with at least some definitions or classification methods. Still the Census is the only game in town. It should be recalled that the civil servants who design the Census do not have prior knowledge of the kinds of information people will want later on, thus it often spreads out the entire deck, printing long rows of figures which you can recompute and combine for your own purposes. For example, the Census divides its income figures for the borough of Brooklyn into 15 categories (Table II.1).

It is entirely up to you to decide whether you want to telescope some of the Census' categories when you put their figures in your own tables. For example, the $15,000 to $24,999 range is the "largest" one for Brooklyn (103,663 households) because the Census editors chose to print incomes in the $10,000 to $14,999 range on two lines (81,014 and 83,412) rather than as a single statistic (which would have been 164,426). Moreover, because of their decision you will never be able to know how many of the 103,663 households between $15,000 and $24,999 fall in the $15,000 to $20,000 bracket and how many have incomes between $20,000 and $24,999. In other words, sometimes the Census gives you too much information and sometimes it

158

158 APPENDIX II

Table II.1. Income of Households in Brooklyn, 1970
(families plus individuals living alone)

$50,000 and over	3,475	1%
$25,000 to $49,999	22,336	3%
$15,000 to $24,999	103,663	15%
$12,000 to $14,999	83,412	12%
$10,000 to $11,999	81,014	12%
$9,000 to $9,999	42,259	6%
$8,000 to $8,999	46,871	7%
$7,000 to $7,999	46,208	7%
$6,000 to $6,999	46,793	7%
$5,000 to $5,999	45,661	7%
$4,000 to $4,999	40,344	6%
$3,000 to $3,999	38,598	5%
$2,000 to $2,999	34,121	5%
$1,000 to $1,999	20,850	3%
Under $1,000	29,923	4%
	685,528	100%

refuses to publish just the statistics you most want. Given their figures for Brooklyn incomes, you are free to arrange them as you please. Depending on the story you want to tell, you could create figures as disparate as those depicted here. There is nothing wrong with selecting your own emphasis so long as you let your readers know that the figures allow for varying interpretations. (The Census does not usually supply percentages; you will have to compute them yourself.)

Do not expect many cross-tabulations, as far as city populations are concerned. The Census will not tell you, for example, the various educational levels of people in each of their income ranges. Thus you can easily discover that Rochester, New York has 295 households with incomes over $50,000; but they are not cross-classified by level of schooling, so we will never know how many of those 295 are college graduates and how many are self-made individuals. When the Census does print cross-tabulations it is usually by race. So if you are interested, you can find out how many of Rochester's $50,000 households are headed by blacks (11 of the 295). On occasion, however, the Census will provide some fairly full breakdowns. For example in one *Subject Report,* the people who have recently moved out of cities into

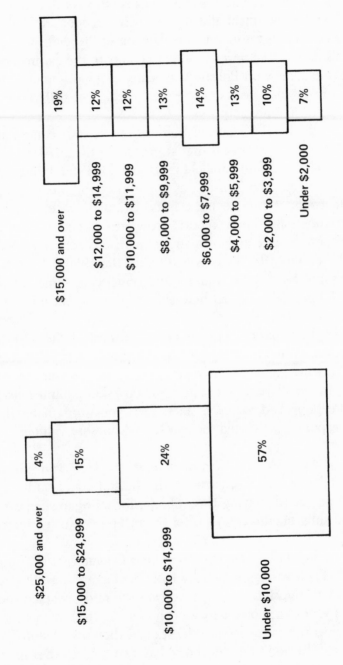

INCOME DISTRIBUTION AMONG BROOKLYN HOUSEHOLDS

(Source: 1970 Census)

nearby suburbs are broken down by age, education, occupation, and family income. But just because this is done in one publication does not mean it will be repeated in another. Thus no report gives figures for income breakdowns of "foreign stock" individuals, so you will never be able to compare the earnings of Italian–Americans with Polish–Americans. A good rule of thumb about cross-tabulations is not to expect much, but still to keep your eye open for some surprises.

Since 1960 Census publications have become fairly standardized, which means that after reading the 1970 reports you can go back and find parallel tabulations for 1960. However, in 1950 and earlier, the Census was much more rudimentary and tended to confine itself to basic information on race, education, and occupations. Those reports are worth inspecting, but don't expect to be able to draw many comparisons between, say, 1930 and 1970. The 1980 Census will follow the 1960–1970 format, publishing a few new volumes and remedying some old omissions. The guidelines given here should prove applicable for 1980.

Four basic documents contain most of the information on cities. (The Census prefers to call them "places" because some cities are unincorporated and prints special columns for all places with populations exceeding 50,000.) The volumes listed below are published for each state, so if you want material on Minneapolis, you should look in the Minnesota volume.

PC(1)A *Number of Inhabitants.* Here you simply get the total population of each city in the state, and nothing more. It is not worth buying this volume, for its figures appear again in all subsequent reports, often in an updated or corrected form.

PC(1)B *General Population Characteristics.* This volume starts off with tables giving basic demographic statistics for each city in the state. Age breakdowns are fairly detailed (how many 14 year olds, how many 75 through 79, etc.), with each of these categories cross-classified by sex and then into "white" and "Negro." In addition, the book has two tables covering domestic matters such as the number of families with and without children, where a woman heads the household, and the marital, nonmarital, and former marital status of everyone over 14. (For New York City all of this information is also given separately for each borough.)

PC(1)C   *General Social and Economic Characteristics.* Anyone intent on studying a city will end up spending most of his time with this volume. Its tables touch on nearly a hundred social and economic characteristics which are, in turn, divided into subcategories. Thus level of schooling has 10 possibilities, ranging from none at all to graduate study. Country of origin for "foreign stock" residents gives 29 places, from Norway to "not reported." There are headings for Mother Tongue ("language spoken in the person's house when he was a child"), State of Birth, Year Moved into Present House, Veteran Status, Means of Transportation to Work, Place of Employment, Income, Family Composition, and Female Fertility ("number of children ever born per 1,000 women ever married"). This is only a sampling. Each city got six pages of figures in the 1970 volume, and cities with substantial black or Hispanic populations get additional tables giving the same information, but only for those individuals.

PC(1)D   *Detailed Characteristics.* Considering its promising title, this volume is a great disappointment. The "details" offered use age as their principal cross-classification. Thus one can discover, for a city, how many of its white foreign-born women are between 15 and 19 years old or how many of its native-born male residents between 30 and 34 were born outside the state where they currently reside. Two further tables give additional breakdowns on national origin and mother tongue, cross-tabulating these with race. Thus New York has 18 people who were born in Denmark and are classed as "non-white." Despite its title, the volume supplies no further details on income, education, employment, or marital arrangements. It does, in its closing tables, give fairly complete information on persons who fall below the poverty line. Thus one can analyze a city's low-income population in terms of age, race, and family composition. The only difficulty is that the "poverty line" verges on malnutrition. To be "poor" at the time of the 1970 Census an urban family of four could not have an income exceeding $3,743. At that level we are, in fact, talking about the *very* poor, or those really at the bottom of the economic barrel. (It should be added that the Census Bureau itself did not invent the precise cutoff points which place people above or below the poverty line. Those figures, we are told, came out of a "Federal Interagency Committee.")

About three years after the Census has been taken, PC(1)A, PC(1)B, PC(1)C, and PC(1)D are reprinted together in large clothbound books entitled *Characteristics of the Population.* Until then, you have to use the separate paperbound reports. (In fact, you may want to continue to use them, as they are cheaper and much easier to copy from due to their more flexible bindings.)

The Census issues almost 40 *Subject Reports* under the prefix PC(2). These give detailed information on a wide variety of topics ranging from "Women by Number of Children Ever Born" to "Occupations of Persons with High Earnings." However, only nine of the Subject Reports issued for 1970 supply separate breakdowns for cities. They are:

PC(2) 1B   *Negro Population.* Information on social, economic, and demographic characteristics for the black residents of the 46 cities with black populations numbering at least 50,000. In 1960 this report was designated PC(2)1C.

PC(2) 1C   *Persons of Spanish Origin.* Information on social, economic, and demographic characteristics for individuals of Hispanic ancestry in the 30 cities with Hispanic populations numbering at least 25,000. For 20 of these cities special columns are provided for Mexican–Americans; for four Puerto Ricans have separate tabulations; and in three residents of Cuban origin have their own columns. This report was not issued in 1960.

PC(2) 1D   *Persons of Spanish Surname.* Information on social, economic, and demographic characteristics for persons with Spanish surnames in 21 cities in Arizona, California, Colorado, New Mexico, and Texas. In 1960 this report was designated PC(2)1B.

PC(2) 1E   *Puerto Ricans in the United States.* Information
on social, economic, and demographic characteristics for individuals who themselves or whose parents were born in Puerto
Rico and are now living in the 16 mainland cities with a Puerto
Rican population numbering at least 5,000. In 1960 this report
was designated PC(2)1D.

PC(2) 1G   *Japanese, Chinese, and Filipinos in the United
States.* Information on social, economic, and demographic characteristics for persons of Japanese, Chinese, or Filipino ancestry
in the 11 cities with Japanese, Chinese, or Filipino populations
numbering at least 5,000. Tabulations of individuals of Chinese
origin have been done for nine of these cities, on Japanese for
eight, and on Filipinos for seven. This report did not appear in
1960.
    Note: from these reports you can find out how many Filipi-
nos in a city have completed college or how many Cuban–Americans have incomes between $10,000 and $15,000. However, no
such social or economic information is published for the people
we customarily think of as "white." Even if you subtract all the
blacks, Chinese, Japanese, Filipinos, Puerto Ricans, Cubans,
Mexican–Americans, and others with Spanish surnames from the
total population of a city, the remainder will contain Arabs,
Thais, Koreans, American Indians, plus others of unreported or
indeterminate origin. As a result, Census reports do not divide in
such a way as to permit a complete ethnic catalog of a city.

PC(2) 2C   *Mobility for Metropolitan Areas.* The tables in
this report tend to be difficult to work out. They give the number
and characteristics of the persons who moved both in and out of
cities and their surrounding areas during the five years preceding
the Census. Thus one discovers that the adults who moved into
New York City between 1965 and 1970 actually contained a
higher proportion of college graduates (39 percent) than did
those moving to the territory just outside the city (26 percent).
There is also material on age, education, race, and occupations
for comers, goers, and stayers, but the figures on income are
computed rather deceptively and should be used with caution.
This report had the same designation in 1960.

PC(2) 4E   *Persons in Institutions and Other Group Quarters.* Information on social, economic, and demographic characteristics for individuals residing in prisons, dormitories, hospitals, and military bases in cities having at least 1,000 persons living under such auspices. In 1960 this report was designated PC(2)8A.

PC(2) 6D   *Journey to Work.* While this report is too heavy (six and a half pounds and 1,170 pages) to take to bed, it makes excellent light reading. Take San Francisco. You can discover how many of its residents also work in the city and how many travel to jobs outside. The 166,831 persons who commute into San Francisco on a typical day are classified by where they come from. Nearby San Mateo County contributes 62,918, but 235 come all the way up from Long Beach and 191 arrive from New York City. Another table gives the sex, age, race, education, occupation, and income of people according to whether they work in the city or travel outside to their jobs. Thus the San Franciscan who both lives and works in the city has a median income of $6,220, whereas his nextdoor neighbor who journeys to a job in Berkeley earns $7,832. (The rolling stone gets more moss—$1,612 more.) Among those who live in San Francisco, 30,463 walk to their jobs. In Milwaukee, which has about the same population, only 19,975 do. When read with care, this report gives some unexpected insights into the flavor of a city. In 1960 it was designated PC(2)6B.

PC(2) 9B   *Low Income Areas in Large Cities.* Information on social, economic, and demographic characteristics of the residents of 50 large cities who happen to live in Census Tracts where 20 percent or more of the inhabitants have incomes below the poverty line. This does not mean that everyone included in these tabulations has a low income. It only means that their home happens to be located in a Census Tract where at least one person in five has been defined as "poor" by the standards mentioned earlier. (A Census Tract consists of a cluster of about six or seven city blocks.) New York City has 2,089,518, or 39 percent of its overall population, living in "low income areas" although, to repeat, not all these people are themselves poor. Milwaukee has

131,611, or 19 percent of its residents, in such areas. These figures have only a limited use, as they fail to distinguish poor people from the nonpoor people who live near them. The report was not published in 1960.

CITIES AND "SUBURBS" ACCORDING TO THE CENSUS

The Census's favorite geographical division is not the city but rather an artifact of its own devising: the "Standard Metropolitan Statistical Area." An SMSA consists of a "central city" (or in some cases, "twin cities" such as Minneapolis and St. Paul) having at least 50,000 people, plus the surrounding county or counties which are "socially and economically integrated" with the central city. The 1970 Census has 243 SMSAs, ranging from the one for Meriden, Connecticut (55,959) to New York City's (11,571,899). All in all, Census publications give more breakdowns and tabulations for SMSAs than they do for the cities themselves. For example, they will tell you how many American Indians are employed in clerical jobs in the Chicago SMSA as a whole, but they do not supply that figure for Chicago by itself. Similarly, they print out the state of birth for everyone in the Philadelphia SMSA, but this information is not provided for the people living just within the city.

We do live in a metropolitan generation and plainly have use for figures which conjoin cities with their outlying regions. The problems arise with the Census's conception of *outlying regions*. It is critical to bear in mind that the noncity portion of an SMSA *always* consists of an *entire* county or counties, not simply the suburban fringe that rings the city. Thus it is inaccurate to refer to the noncity portion of an SMSA as its "suburbs." The outer part obviously contains some suburbs, but it embraces a lot more as well. For instance, the SMSA for Denver includes four surrounding counties in their entirety, including Jefferson County, which stretches 30 miles to the south, and Adams County extending 60 miles northeast into a virtually uninhabited area. The Census's view of *metropolitan* Tucson takes in all of Pima County, which runs for 150 miles across Arizona and exceeds New Hampshire in size.

So many counties have been appended to the SMSAs of most larger cities that the urban portion looks like a beleaguered enclave. Cleveland itself now accounts for only 36 percent of its SMSA population. Boston's share is a mere 23 percent. New York's case is equally perplexing, but in a different way. The New York City SMSA contains the city's five boroughs, plus Nassau and Suffolk counties on Long Island, Westchester to the north, and Rockland County on the west bank of the Hudson River. Strangely, no parts of New Jersey are included in New York's SMSA even though that state sent 192,588 commuters into the city every day, more than the combined total coming from Westchester, Rockland, and Suffolk Counties. Indeed, New Jersey's Bergen County is geographically closer to New York City than is Rockland County and provides four times as many commuters. Due to the Jersey omissions, the New York City SMSA presents a distorted picture of "metropolitan" New York.

The fact that Bergen County is in another state is not the problem; the Census frequently puts counties from two or more states in an SMSA. The real trouble is that a lot of New Jersey's counties are contained in SMSAs of their own, such as the one for Paterson–Clifton–Passaic. This apparently disqualifies them from being in New York City's SMSA as well. The Census does have a special "New York–Northeastern New Jersey Standard Consolidated Area" which held 16,178,700 people in 1970. Unfortunately it errs on the side of generosity, reaching almost to Trenton.

The Census does have a much more realistic category it calls the "Urbanized Area." This includes a central city, along with just those surrounding communities we normally think of as suburbs. Contrast, for example, Baltimore's SMSA with its "Urbanized Area" in Table II.2.

Table II.2.

SMSA			Urbanized Area	
905,759	44%	within central city	905,759	57%
1,164,911	56	outside central city	674,022	43
2,070,670	100%		1,579,781	100%

In this case the Urbanized Area's noncity portion represents suburban Baltimore more accurately than does the noncity segment of the SMSA. Anyone wishing to compare the characteristics of city-dwellers and suburbanites would be well advised to use the Urbanized Area figures for a city and to forget about the SMSA statistics altogether. (Unfortunately there is no Urbanized Area for New York City.)

The Census publishes four additional *Subject Reports* which give tabulations for SMSAs. These volumes do not include breakdowns for Urbanized Areas, nor do they supply separate columns for the city portions of the SMSAs. Thus you can find, say, educational information for people of various national ancestries in an SMSA, but it will not tell you how many of them live within the city and how many reside in the outlying counties. These reports are:

PC(2)1A   *National Origin and Language.* Information on social, economic, and demographic characteristics for "foreign stock" persons in 22 selected SMSAs. In 1960 this report appeared in two separate volumes, designated PC(2)1A and PC(2)1E.

PC(2)1F   *American Indians.* Information on social, economic, and demographic characteristics for American Indians in the 30 SMSAs with Indian populations numbering at least 2,500. This report did not appear in 1960.

PC(2)2A   *State of Birth.* Information on social and economic characteristics of persons in the 125 largest SMSAs, cross-tabulated by the state in which they were born. This report had the same designation in 1960.

PC(2)2E   *Migration Between State Economic Areas.* The Census divides the entire country up into 510 "State Economic Areas." Some are rural or cover small towns, but in the most densely populated regions the SMSAs do double service as State Economic Areas. The tables in this volume indicate where the in-migrants to an SMSA came from and where its out-migrants went to during the five years prior to the taking of the Census.

Thus the Minneapolis SMSA received 266 New Hampshire residents and shipped 265 of its people over to New Hampshire. The report gets even more detailed, showing how many persons Atlanta's SMSA got from Iowa's Pottawattamie County (33) or how many it sent to Bexar County in Texas (790). It would, of course, be useful to know the origins and destinations of people moving in and out of the cities. However, for reasons best known to itself, the Census declines to publish such information for centers such as Detroit or Philadelphia or New York City even though it gives full figures on all the comings and goings from Pottawattamie County. This is another instance of where the Census's fixation on its SMSA precludes giving information in other forms. This report had the same designation in 1960.

HC(1)B *Detailed Housing Characteristics.* The Census also publishes reports in which "housing units" (homes, apartments, single rooms) comprise the basic data. While the tabulations indicate how many human beings live in each dwelling, its figures on possessions such as dishwashers, food freezers, and portable radios apply to how many are owned per household and not by each person. The basic statistics deal with number of rooms, kind of fuel and plumbing facilities, rent paid, estimated market value, and age of the structure. At first glance the volume seems merely to describe the physical side of the city. But small items begin to shed a more human light. Syracuse, for example, has 22 families who use wood for their heating fuel. Forty-two of Buffalo's 988 Puerto Rican households share their bath or shower with another family. On the other hand, 124,732 of New York City's families, of which 11,339 were black, own a second home. This report had the same designation in 1960.

PHC(1) *Census Tracts.* The Census does best by the cities in printing sets of figures for small areas it calls "Tracts." No less than 241 cities, Abilene to Youngstown, go through this regimen. So far as the tabulations are concerned, the people living in each Tract are treated as if they were an independent village. Take, for example, Tract 366 in the Gun Hill Road section of the northeast Bronx. A total of 783 individuals live on its eight blocks. The Census tells us that 5 of them walk to work, 10 have completed college, 94 are first- or second-generation Italians, and 433 reside in the same house they lived in five years earlier. New York City is divided up into 2,199 Tracts. Another 39 cities need at least 100 to cover their territory. You can use the Tracts just as you would tiny jigsaw puzzle pieces, as you proceed to divide up the city by creating your own districts or neighborhoods. (State legislatures use the Tracts to make up electoral constituencies.) A map comes with each Tract volume, but it is a very simplified one. You will need to have a more detailed city map on hand to make sure you have the precise locations of the tracts you are using. Anyone using tracts should be forewarned: adding up figures tract by tract is an arduous business and very hard on the eyes. The Census retains the same tracts year after year even if homes are torn down and the residential population reduced to almost nil. Tract Number 9 in Lower Manhattan contains exactly 16 people, of whom (the Census reports) seven are married, seven are single, and two are divorced.

SOME PROBLEMS AND PRECAUTIONS

Black or White? Suppose you would like to know how many black, white, and Hispanic individuals live in a particular city. Unfortunately Census figures cannot give you a precise answer. For Philadelphia, for example, the Census has figures on the number of black and Puerto Rican residents in the city. The difficulty is that some Puerto Ricans are also black, or at least identify themselves as such; so those persons are counted twice, once in the Puerto Rican tabulations and once in the black listings. If you wish to eliminate that duplication, you would have to remove the black Puerto Ricans from the black column. However, the Census, for some reason, refuses to give a racial breakdown for the Puerto Ricans of Philadelphia or any other city. For the country as a whole, the Census does say that about 5 percent of Puerto Ricans are black and about 2 percent are Indian. (The same proportions apply for persons of other Hispanic origins, as well.) But you have no way of knowing whether the national percentages hold in Philadelphia, so if you wish to create separate categories for the black and Hispanic populations of a city, you will have to content yourself with estimates.

Not All in the Family. Some people live by themselves; the Census calls them "unrelated individuals." Other people live in conventional father-mother-children households; the Census calls them "families." However, there are a lot of other ways to live. If two or more relatives of any kind reside together they are also included in the "family" category. For example, two sisters or a mother with children or grandparents plus a grandchild. In other instances, two or more "unrelated" individuals share a house or apartment. In such cases their incomes are classified as if they lived under entirely separate roofs. Thus when four young women share an apartment they are treated as four distinct households, as if each had her own apartment. Or take the situation in which Mary and John have been living together perhaps for several years with Mary earning $15,000 and John $12,000. Were they married, the Census would list them as a single $27,000 family. But because they are not, Mary is listed with all the other single people who earn $15,000, while John goes in with those making $12,000. So there are, especially in larger cities, more multisalary, and hence higher-income, homes than the Census figures suggest. In fact, the Census will not tell us how many unwedded couples there are living together, in individual cities or for the country as a whole.

Who's New in Town? For everyone five years old or older, the Census asks where they were living five years earlier. Among those who resided outside the city five years before, the Census gives figures for how many were living in a different state or abroad and how many were living in the same state but in a county different from the one in which the city is situated. All this is in the volume, *Social and Economic Characteristics.* In addition, the volume, *Mobility for Metropolitan Areas,* lists the number of people who arrived in the city from one or another of the counties in the city's SMSA. So with Denver, for example, one can distinguish in-migrants from far-off Grand Junction from those who simply moved into the city from suburban Littleton. Problems arise, however, with New York or any other city that happens to contain more than one county within its boundaries. The Census tells us that New York City had in 1970 a total of 658,188 persons who lived in a different county of New York State in 1965. Of these, 66,837 had resided in Nassau, Westchester, Rockland, or Suffolk Counties. What about the remaining 591,351? Some of them, probably the great majority, had simply shifted counties within New York City itself: like moving from Brooklyn (Kings County) to Staten Island (Richmond County). Others had moved to New York from upstate counties such as Monroe (which contains Rochester) or Onondaga (Syracuse). But the Census does not separate intercounty movers who simply move within the city from individuals who migrate from counties beyond the metropolitan area. The reason for this negligence is that the Census uses a single publication format for every city, always using "different county" regardless of whether it is a single-county city or a multicounty city. Multicounty cities should have separate tabulations for people who lived in a different county within the city and those whose county of origin was outside the city.

Apples and Oranges. What follows now is a short case study in how Census classification methods can prevent you from obtaining information you might want to have. Suppose you wish to know the ethnic composition of everyone in Chicago who earns between $10,000 and $14,999. You go to the various *Special Report* volumes which have figures for black, Mexican–American, Chinese, Japanese, Filipino, and Puerto Rican persons in Chicago. Adding these together, you determine that the city contains 39,609 individuals of these ancestries with incomes in the $10,000 to $14,999 range. Therefore, you have only to subtract 39,609 from the total number of Chicagoans, and you will have the figure for whites in that income bracket. (That residual figure will also contain some Turks, Thais, Cubans, Koreans, and American Indians but not enough to affect the proportion in a serious way.) But you then discover that the Census does not give the total number of *people* in Chicago who earn between $10,000 and $14,999. What it does tell you, in its tables on *General Social and Economic Characteristics,* is that 234,148 of its families and 30,510 of the city's unrelated individuals have incomes in that range. But you cannot subtract 39,609 people from 234,148 families and 30,510 individuals. Some of those families will certainly have had two or more earners with lower incomes which brought the household total up to $10,000 or more. So such a family is not comparable to a single person earning an equal amount. In other words the Census uses apples (income per person) for its ethnic reports and oranges (income per family and unrelated individuals) for its overall tabulations. This may seem a wearisome story, but it illustrates the kind of roadblock one can encounter when trying to develop his own computations and finds that the Census figures work at cross-purposes to him.

Tapes. If you have a lot of money and easy access to a computer, much of what has been said here will have been wasted on you. For the Census will sell you a magnetic tape containing all the statistics on your city; then you can run any tabulations you like. If you want to know how many Filipino automobile mechanics in San Diego are married to Chicano nurses, just refer to the codebook and push the appropriate buttons. The only problem with this method is that it tends to suppress serendipity. Browsing through the actual tables can suggest possible correlations and combinations that had not occurred to you before you started thumbing. As suggested earlier, some of the Census volumes make excellent bedtime reading.

Notes

CHAPTER 1: Introducing Eight Million People

1. Emanuel S. Savas, "Information Systems in a New York Urban Observatory," *Socio-Economic Planning Sciences*, vol. 1, (1968), pp. 203–204.

2. Jerome B. Wiesner, *Hearings* before the Subcommittee on Executive Reorganization of the Committee on Government Operations, United States Senate, 90th Congress, First Session, Washington, D.C.: U. S. Government Printing Office, 1967, p. 3,275.

3. Britton Harris, "The New Technology and Urban Planning," *Urban Affairs Quarterly*, vol. 3, (1967), p. 27.

4. Melville Branch, "Simulation, Mathematical Models, and Comprehensive City Planning," *Urban Affairs Quarterly*, vol. 1, (1966), p. 27. By permission of the publishers, Sage Publications, Inc.

5. Savas, "Information Systems," p. 203.

6. Morton Hunt, *Sexual Behavior in the 1970's*, Chicago: Playboy Press, 1974, p. 190.

7. Banfield, *The Unheavenly City Revisited*, Boston: Little, Brown, 1974, p. 61.

CHAPTER 2: A Portrait in Percentages

1. Full tables with ethnic breakdowns are printed in Appendix I which details some assumptions that have to be made in collating information on race and national origins. For example, there is some duplication in the figures for blacks and Puerto Ricans; also, the "white" totals include Asians and some Hispanics.

CHAPTER 3: The City's Politics

1. The city has voters who apparently make a point of supporting a major party candidate on a minor party line when he has both designations. Between 109,462 Liberals (in the case of McGovern in 1972) and 218,687 (with Humphrey four years earlier) have chosen not to swell the Democratic showing. In 1968 no fewer than

317,930 voters supported Jacob Javits as a Liberal in preference to his Republican affiliation. By the same token, 212,905 of Marchi's 1969 votes came on the Conservative line; however only 154,361 voters decided to back Nixon as a Conservative. There is a message in this mode of voting; it tells the major parties that the voter's basic loyalties lie elsewhere and that they have his support only as long as they nominate acceptable candidates.

2. In contrast, North Harlem had an incidence of robberies reaching 320 per 10,000 householders, yet only 17 percent of its voters sided with the police position. Central Harlem drew only 20 percent for abolition of the review board, even with 599 robberies for every 10,000 residents. Bedford-Stuyvesant, Brownsville, and the South Bronx had similar ratios. Obviously people living in those neighborhoods wanted and needed more safety. They may have had mixed feelings about whether civilian review would hamper the effectiveness of the police. But they also found police deportment toward law-abiding citizens sufficiently obnoxious to risk lowering police efficiency if they could thereby gain an agency for their own complaints. Voters in slum sections had a hard choice because they felt beset from both sides. They feared the criminals in their midst, yet they had no confidence at all in the police who were supposed to protect them. (It should not be necessary to add that the average mugger or addict does not participate in elections.)

3. Arthur Klebanoff puts most of the blame on the professional politicians. "The political leadership in this town doesn't want more registered voters because they prefer small, controllable constituencies," he was quoted as saying in the New York Times, January 13, 1974. This reluctance explains why black and Latin district leaders do little to encourage voting in their areas. Still, the fact remains that many more whites will register and vote on their own volition, often quite oblivious to the opinions of neighborhood politicians.

CHAPTER 4: A City of Communities?

1. Sayre and Kaufman, Governing New York City, New York: Norton, 1960, p. 28.

2. Quoted in Jewel Bellush, "Housing: The Scatter-Site Controversy," in Jewel Bellush and Stephen M. David, eds., Race and Politics in New York City, New York: Praeger, 1971, p. 122.

3. New York City Planning Commission, Plan for New York City: A Proposal Cambridge: MIT Press, 1969, vol. 1, p. 126.

4. Breslin, "The Political Discovery of the Year," New York (November 3, 1969), p. 33.

5. New York Times, August 6 and 23, September 20, October 19 and 31, 1969; March 11 and 27, April 2, May 16, 1970.

6. New York City Planning Commission, Plan for New York City, pp. 126–32.

7. New York Times, April 10, 1972.

8. Quoted in Suzanne Keller, The Urban Neighborhood, New York: Vintage Books, 1968, p. 7.

9. Cook, "Cultural Innovation and Disaster in the American City," in Leonard J. Duhl, ed., The Urban Condition, New York: Clarion, 1969, p. 88.

10. Alumni Directory, Princeton: Princeton Univ. Press, 1969.

11. New York Times, February 11, 1970.

12. *Ibid.*, March 16, 1970.

13. *Manhattan Tribune*, November 29, 1969.

14. "Around City Hall," *New Yorker* (February 28, 1970).

15. *Daily News*, November 16, 1969.

16. *Rockaway Journal*, December 23, 1969.

17. *New York Times*, January 31, 1970.

18. *Kings Courier*, December 20, 1969.

19. *Daily News*, October 26, 1969.

20. Lindsay, *The City*, New York: Norton, 1970, p. 130.

21. *Kings Courier*, December 20, 1969.

22. *New York Times*, February 11, 1970.

23. *Ibid.*, November 9, 1969.

24. Earl Raab, "What War and Which Poverty?" *Public Interest* (Spring 1966), p. 52.

25. A not atypical assembly district might contain pieces of three state senate districts, two congressional districts, two city council districts, and four municipal court districts. Consequently, citizens find themselves aligned with a different set of fellow constituents in virtually every balloting.

26. A three-page proposal by a group calling itself "Citizens for Local Democracy" began with the statement, "we must divide the metropolis into some 50 communities, each with local control of local institutions, each with its own democratic political structure." (*New York Review* [October 22, 1970].) However, the prospectus goes on to inform these not-yet-instituted communities that they should each have a "town square," complete with swimming pool, art center, and six cafes. Apparently the authors could not bring themselves to say: "we live on the Upper West Side, and this is what we would like to do with *our* neighborhood. And you should be able to do with your neighborhood what *you* want to do." Some citizens might prefer a bowling alley to an art center.

27. Lewis, "The Culture of Poverty," *Scientific American*, vol. 215, no. 4., (1960), 25.

28. Marris, "A Report on Urban Renewal in the United States," in Duhl, *Urban Condition*, p. 127.

29. Irelan, *Low-Income Life Styles*, Washington, D.C.: U. S. Government Printing Office, 1966, p. 5.

30. *New York Times*, June 1, 1969.

31. "Fight for Fund Power Perils Anti-Poverty Programs," *Sunday News*, November 30, 1969.

32. Starr, *The Living End*, New York: Coward-McCann, 1966, pp. 272–73.

33. Kaufman, "Bureaucrats and Organized Civil Servants," in Robert H. Connery and Demetrios Caraley, eds., *Governing the City*, New York: Praeger, 1969, p. 48.

34. Decter, letter in *Commentary* (June 1970), p. 18.

35. For a description of the kinds of services district chairmen are still able to render, see "It's Open House for Problems Nightly at Old-Style McManus Political Club," *Sunday News*, September 14, 1969.

36. Glazer and Moynihan, *Beyond the Melting Pot,* 2nd ed., Cambridge: MIT Press, 1970, p. xviii.

37. "An objective view of New York City's government in 1969, comparing it with its own past or with any other large city in the United States or abroad, will reveal that it is among the best governed of the nation's or world's large cities." Wallace Sayre, "City Hall Leadership," in Robert H. Connery and Demetrios Caraley, p. 33.

38. "The intelligentsia, as it so often has, lusted after the sensational and the exotic. The hard work of political and social change bored it. An increasingly dangerous romance with social brinksmanship and violence developed." Glazer and Moynihan, *Beyond the Melting Pot,* p. xvi.

CHAPTER 5: **Classes and Conflict**

1. (These figures are, in fact, lower than welfare allowances provided in New York City. While the federal poverty boundaries approximate welfare stipends, recipients have also their rent paid by the city, and this raises their effective incomes by about $1,500. So many, perhaps most, welfare families would be above the poverty threshold.)

2. S. M. Miller, "The Limits of Social Policy," *New Society* (August 5, 1971), p. 247.

3. Actually several other cities surpass New York in their proportion of population receiving welfare. Tabulations for February 1972 showed that Boston, Baltimore, Philadelphia, and St. Louis all had more people on their public-assistance rolls. *New York Times,* June 15, 1972.

4. Some commentators have argued that black adolescents look forward to early pregnancies, either to ensnare a husband or as a sign of entering adulthood. Yet studies have revealed no little bitterness among those propelled into motherhood. See, for example, Frank F. Furstenberg, "Premarital Pregnancy Among Black Teen-agers," *Transaction* (May 1970), pp. 52–55.

5. *New York Times,* July 5, 1971.

6. Nicholas Kisburg, quoted in the *Daily News,* September 30, 1969.

7. Francis X. Clines, "And if You Find Them, Then What?" *New York Times,* January 14, 1973.

8. *New York Times,* July 12, 1971.

9. James M. Markhan, "The Fight on Narcotics," *New York Times,* February 9, 1973.

10. Orde Coombs, "Fear and Trembling in Black Streets," *New York* (November 20, 1972).

11. In addition, New York has 104,318 Puerto Ricans in this age range. Most white householders, however, still see Hispanic Americans as being less forbidding than blacks, and talk of draconian measures is less apt to be directed at Spanish-speaking citizens.

12. Hunt, *The Mugging,* New York: Atheneum, 1972, p. 63.

13. Lenore E. Bixby, "Income of People Aged 65 and Older: Overview from the 1968 Survey of the Aged," *Social Security Bulletin* (April 1970), pp. 10–11.

14. Rent control has probably saved more of the aged from malnutrition than any other factor. The only problem is that old people are not guaranteed a rent-controlled residence. If a building is torn down or goes up in flames, and along with it their $75

apartment, the erstwhile tenants will have to pay the free-market rate for their new apartment. At the same time, New York has families earning $40,000 a year who pay $175 a month in rent because they were lucky enough to find a rent-controlled building many years ago. Rent control would have some justification if it correlated with ability (or inability) to pay. As matters stand, it is a game of roulette which the well-to-do can win and the late-arriving and dispossessed cannot even enter.

15. Nicholas Kisburg, Irving Levine, Dennis Clark, Whitney Young, and Gus Tyler, quoted in the *New York Times,* April 13, 1969.

16. Carey, quoted in Jimmy Breslin, "The Revolt of the White Lower-Middle Class," *New York* (April 14, 1969).

17. In 1970 the *New York Times* discovered at least one postman whose salary of $6,382 a year put him just $104 ahead of eligibility for welfare benefits. *New York Times,* March 25, 1970.

18. *Ibid.,* November 9, 1970.

19. *Ibid.,* November 30, 1969.

20. Glazer, "Race Relations," in Lyle C. Fitch and Annmarie Walsh, eds., *Agenda for a City,* Beverly Hills: Sage Publications, 1970, pp. 515–16.

21. *New York Times,* October 25, 1970.

22. Pileggi, "Risorgimento: the Red, White, and Greening of New York," *New York* (June 7, 1971), p. 28.

23. Himmelfarb, "Jewish Class Conflict," *Commentary* (January 1970), pp. 37–42.

24. Halberstam, "The Very Expensive Education of McGeorge Bundy," *Harpers* (July 1969), p. 39.

25. Holden, *The Republican Crisis,* San Francisco: Chandler, 1972, p. 73.

26. *New York Times,* May 29, 1973.

27. Quoted in Raymond Vernon, *The Myth and Reality of Our Urban Problems,* Cambridge: Joint Center for Urban Studies, 1962, p. 30.

28. Circulation analysis, January 24, 1972.

29. For the origins and educations of corporation heads see the tabulations in James Reichley, "Our Critical Shortage of Leadership," *Fortune* (September 1971), p. 91.

30. *New York Times,* February 5, 1971.

31. *Ibid.,* June 27, 1971. In addition, religious schools enroll approximately 365,000 pupils, of whom about 85 percent are in schools affiliated with the Catholic dioceses of New York City.

CHAPTER 6: **Not Just Another City**

1. Lindsay, *The City,* New York: Norton, 1970, p. 50.

2. Lyford, Hearings before the Subcommittee on Executive Reorganization of the Committee on Government Operations, United States Senate, 90th Congress, First Session, Washington, D.C.: U.S. Government Printing Office, 1967, p. 1,135.

3. *New York Times,* December 17, 1972.

178

4. *Ibid.*, January 14, 1974. In the fall of 1971 only 20 percent of my Queens College students said they would like to be living in New York City 15 years after their graduation. By the spring of 1974, the proportion wishing to remain in the city had risen to 38 percent.

5. The time will probably come when these conditions will no longer beset the city, but that will result not from public programs or increased expenditures and certainly not from some chimera called "leadership." (New Yorkers have ceased being the sort of people who will follow anyone.) Most of the city's troubles stem from the presence of persons whose everyday actions make life hazardous for those around them. No one predicted the emergence of this kind of conduct, nor did anyone foresee that it would take such destructive proportions. Circumstances such as the introduction of heroin, the rise in vandalism, and the upsurge of illegitimacy came unanticipated by social analysts. If the number of addicts, derelicts, and other undesirables diminishes over the coming generation, their disappearance will stem not from well-wrought laws or intelligent administration, but rather from new combinations of events which produce new patterns of conduct.

6. Edward B. Banfield and James Q. Wilson, *City Politics,* New York: Vintage, 1963, p. 344.

7. Whalen, *A City Destroying Itself,* New York: Morrow, 1965, p. 12.

8. Elazar, "Are We a Nation of Cities?" *Public Interest* (Summer 1966), p. 48.

9. I asked the students in my Queens College introductory course how frequently they visited Manhattan. More than half of them made the trip less than twice a month.

10. "The Metropolitanites," *Fortune* (July 1939), p. 84.

11. San Francisco's range of amenities results chiefly from the very large number of out-of-town visitors who make a much-expanded clientele. It remains problematic how many of these activities the city's 715,674 residents themselves could support.

12. Norman Mailer, "Why Are We in New York?" in Peter Manso, ed., *Running Against the Machine,* Garden City: Doubleday, 1969, p. 9.

13. Kristol, "It's Not Such a Bad Crisis to Live In," *New York Times Magazine* (January 22, 1967), p. 70.

14. If the city becomes composed principally of people who want to live there, it doesn't much matter whether its white component is 60 percent or 35 percent or even 15 percent of the population. One characteristic of a modern city-dweller must be unconcern about the color of those living around him. An affinity for the urban life should be an attitude transcending race. (Many suburbanites no longer visit the city because they are made uncomfortable by the sight of so many hued faces on the streets or in the shops. This seldom bothers resident New Yorkers who tend to take such matters in their stride.)

15. Dahl, "The City in the Future of Democracy," *American Political Science Review* (December 1967), p. 958.

16. Mumford, Hearings before Subcommittee on Executive Reorganization, ibid., p. 3,614.

17. Suburban communities prefer not to absorb their quotient of the poor, with the result that New York must provide homes and services for a greater concentration of individuals with low incomes. In housing and looking after these people, the city is, in effect, doing Scarsdale and Short Hills a favor—a boon seldom acknowledged and never reciprocated.

Index

179